W9-CML-891

Windows Westward

Windows Westward

ROME, RUSSIA, REUNION

Very Rev. Stephen C. Gulovich, Ph.D., S.T.D.

New York

THE DECLAN X. McMULLEN COMPANY

Nihil obstat

Rev. Michael A. Knapik

Imprimatur

✠Daniel Ivancho

Episcopus titularis Europi, administer apostolicus Exarchatus Pittsburghensis ritus byzantino-slavi

MUNHALL, PENNSYLVANIA
Die 22 februarii, 1947

MANUFACTURED IN THE U. S. A.

Dedicated to

THE MOST REVEREND BASIL TAKACH, D.D.

Titular Bishop of Zela

FIRST ORDINARY OF THE PITTSBURGH CATHOLIC
EXARCHATE OF THE BYZANTINE-SLAVONIC RITE

PREFACE

THIS study is not offered as an exhaustive treatment of the Byzantine-Slavonic Rite. It limits itself to discussing this rite in its most important phases. Mindful of the words of Pius XI, "To unite we must above all know each other," I point to those facts and events in the long history of the rite which are of special significance and can serve as focal points for further study. The present book should be read in connection with such valuable books in English on the Eastern Rites as those by Dr. Adrian Fortescue, Donald Attwater, and others mentioned in the appended bibliography.

In the past ten years I have come across many statements that are apt to mislead those not familiar with the past of the Byzantine-Slavonic Rite. There is an abundance of material through which the English-speaking public has not been presented with a full or honest presentation of the facts. Others, as well as I, have suffered much from such an approach. Correspondence with many sincere seekers for an accurate picture and conversation after numerous and countrywide lecture tours have led me to seek to satisfy those who wish to look further into the evolution of the rites in the bosom of the Church and their relations with the Holy See, and who have sought a brief and helpful guidebook.

I have tried to put forward in this work nothing more than statements of fact. What few conclusions I draw are, I am convinced, well substantiated by the facts. My main intention has been to arouse in my readers a desire to seek the sources and ascertain the truth.

I am grateful to all who cooperated with me in this endeavor and made the publication of this book possible. In particular I wish to thank the editors of *The American Ecclesiastical Review* for permission to reprint a substantial portion from the *Memorandum* of Dr. Vladimir Soloviev, and the Catholic Near East Welfare Association for its enthusiastic interest in these essays.

Acknowledgment also is due to the following publishers: Burns, Oates and Washbourne, Ltd., for permission to quote from Adrian Fortescue, *The Uniate Eastern Church;* E. P. Dutton & Co., Inc., for permission to quote from V. O. Kluchevsky, *A History of Russia;* Sheed & Ward, Inc., for selections from J. N. Danzas, *The Russian Church,* and from Erik and Christine von Kuhnelt-Leddihn, *The Gates of Hell.*

CONTENTS

Windows Westward

I

AN INVITATION

LET us go on an imaginary visit to one of the many Catholic churches of the Byzantine-Slavonic Rite in this country.

As we approach the church, the Byzantine style of architecture promises something different. There stand out strikingly five domes—symbolic of our Lord surrounded by the four evangelists.[1] Sometimes there are as many as twelve, representing the twelve apostles. A triple-bar cross surmounts each of these elongated domes. Authorities do not agree on the symbolism of the triple-bar cross, but a preferred opinion claims that the top bar represents the title

[1] "In architecture . . . the new style of church that remained typical of the later Byzantine development was a cruciform structure with five domes, which may have had its origin in Armenia."—Christopher Dawson, *The Making of Europe* (New York, 1945) 175. In the words of Doctor Golubinsky, one of Russia's ecclesiastical historians, the bulbous steeples we see today represent an eleventh-century modification of the ball which served as a support for the cross surmounting the cupola.

board placed over the head of our Lord, and the bar at the bottom represents the foot rest.

Presently, we enter the vestibule, where in former days the penitents begged the faithful for prayers. On entering the nave we are struck by the absence of statues, by the walls' freedom from the tablets of the Way of the Cross. All we see is that the walls are richly decorated with brightly-colored sacred paintings. We turn our eyes to the sanctuary: it is hidden by a high-reaching wooden screen of fine latticework adorned with rows of ikons. This inspiring structure is the ikonostasis. Behind it, and in the center of the sanctuary, is the flat tablelike altar with its intricately carved tabernacle. A canopy resting on four columns covers the altar. To the left is a smaller altarlike structure known as the prothesis, or table of preparation.

The immense bells begin to toll. The members of the congregation enter the church. It is strange—there is no genuflecting. The faithful make profound bows, extending at the same time their right arm with a sweeping gesture to the floor, as if to place their intelligence and soul at the feet of our Lord in the tabernacle. They also bless themselves differently. The thumb, index, and middle fingers are joined at the tips, symbolizing the Blessed Trinity, while the other two fingers, symbolical or the two natures of Christ, are kept pressed against the palm of the hand. The movement of the sign is not from the left to the right, but vice versa.

Now, our attention is drawn by the incoming procession. A processional cross is borne at its head, followed by candle bearers vested in white. Behind them are two young deacons in dalmatics. A long stole is wound about their breasts, passing under the right armpit and crossed on the left shoulder so as to fall in front and back to their very ankles. Next come the fully vested priests; they show the broad Byzantine stole which reaches the very edge of the alb, and a copelike chasuble—the rich and colorful Byzantine phailonion. Behind them are four clerics—personal attendants to the bishop. Two of them carry specially designed candlesticks—one, a triple candlestick (the trikirion), symbolizing the Blessed Trinity; the other a double candlestick (the dikirion), symbolizing the two natures of Christ.

Following them is the bishop. He is clad in a purple cassock and a broad cape (the mandyas) of the same color, adorned with the images of the four Evangelists. His headgear resembles a royal crown and bears the images of our Lord and the four Evangelists, and is surmounted by a Greek cross. In his hand he carries the pastoral staff. Unlike the Latin crozier, two serpents entwine themselves around it in perfect symmetry to gaze at a globe surmounted by a cross.

The bishop is being vested. First comes the alb and then

the broad Byzantine stole (epitrakhelion). This is followed by the saccos, a garment resembling the deacon's dalmatic, though somewhat shorter and more richly decorated. On his right side is placed a stiff rectangular shield (epigonatikon),[2] symbolizing the shield of faith. And now he puts on the last garment, a long, broad piece of woolen cloth, which is placed upon his shoulder; it resembles a large pallium. This is the omophorion, symbolizing the pastoral dignity of the bishop.

While the bishop is vesting, we notice one priest approaching the prothesis, a small table to the left of the altar in the sanctuary, to which he proceeds with the Proskomedia, the rite of Preparation, in order that the bread and wine used in the Liturgy might be duly prepared.

For a moment everything is hushed and then the solemn voice of the deacon intones, "Bless, O Lord." The Liturgy has begun: an unbroken musical dialogue, between the clergy and the faithful. Even the words of consecration are sung, and answered by the faithful with a majestic long-drawn "Amen." This congregational singing of the sacred chant is considered one of the most beautiful forms of music.

We miss the *Confiteor.* Instead, we hear a long series of

[2] A similar ornament, known as the *subcimtorium,* is used by the Pope.

litanies answered by a melodious response, "Lord have mercy," followed by a series of three antiphons and a magnificent Christological hymn. Suddenly, the sanctuary is alive with action. The deacon ascends the altar and takes into his hands the heavily bound and richly decorated Book of the Gospels. Holding it high over his head, he descends from the altar. Accompanied by the acolytes, subdeacon, and priests, he goes around the altar from right to left, emerging from the side door of the ikonostasis. The entire entourage halts in front of the Royal Doors, the central doors of the ikonostasis, where the deacon calls upon the people to give their undivided attention to the ceremonies about to begin.

The bishop, who all this time was seated on his throne at the right of the ikonostasis, now rises and, accompanied by his personal attendants, comes to the Royal Doors. With the pastoral staff in his left hand, the trikirion in his right hand, he blesses the four corners of the earth. Then the acolytes, deacons, priests, and bishop proceed around the altar three times, singing: "O Son of God, wonderful in Thy saints, save us who sing to Thee, alleluia," while the bishop meantime incenses the altar. Afterwards, the congregation sings: "Come let us adore and fall down before Christ." This is known as the Little Entrance and is really the beginning of the Liturgy. It is a faint remnant of a once magnificent and colorful procession, when, in the early centuries of the Church, the bishop was accompanied to the church by the clergy and notables.

In short order follow the reading of the Epistle and Gospel, another series of litanies which remind us of the *Kyrie* in the Roman ritual and prayers for the catechumens.

While the congregation sings the beautiful Cherubic Hymn, another gem of ancient Christianity, the bishop and clergy leave the altar and halt before the prothesis. The bishop takes the paten with the bread and gives it to the deacon; then he gives the chalice to the senior priest and goes to the foot of the altar. In the meantime, the acolytes and other ministers assisting at the Liturgy form a procession according to their respective ranks. This procession emerges from the left door of the ikonostasis and comes to a halt in front of the Royal Doors where the bishop is waiting to receive from the hands of the deacon and the senior priest the paten and chalice with the bread and wine already prepared for the Holy Sacrifice.

The bishop and clergy now return to the altar. We hear another series of litanies while the bishop recites the prayer of the Offertory. Then the congregation chants the Niceno-Constantinopolitan Creed as the last preparation for the sublime moment that is to come. We hear the *Sursum corda* and the *Gratias agamus Deo,* but, strangely enough, the

Preface is not chanted; instead, the bishop and the co-consecrating priests recite it silently. The congregation breaks forth into the familiar *Sanctus,* but the words of the Consecration are not whispered by the clergy, as we would expect. They are chanted in a majestic monotone to which the congregation responds with a resounding "Amen."[3] There is no elevation after the consecration of each individual element, but when both bread and wine have been consecrated the first deacon takes into his hand the paten with the consecrated bread, the other deacon takes the chalice with the consecrated wine. They raise the Sacred Species crosswise, so as to form with the forearms the letter X.

The saints are invoked and, while the congregation sings a beautiful hymn in honor of the Blessed Mother, professing belief in her divine motherhood, prayers are offered for the living and the dead, and particular mention is made of the Pope, as head of the Church, and of the local diocesan bishop. At the conclusion of the Canon we hear another series of litanies which introduce the familiar Lord's Prayer chanted by the congregation.

[3] This, apparently, was also the custom in the West. In a sermon before the bishops at the Council of Agde (506), St. Caesarius of Arles said among other things: "You can read the books of the prophets, the writings of the Apostles, and even the Gospels, *but the Consecration you can only hear and see in the house of God.*" Cf. J. J. Guiniven, C.SS.R., *The Precept of Hearing Mass* (Washington, 1942), 24.

We now witness the ceremonies connected with Holy Communion. The bishop breaks the Sacred Host and gives to each concelebrating priest and to the deacons a particle of the Sacred Body. When this is consumed, the priests and the deacons, one by one, sip a portion of the Precious Blood from the chalice. In the meantime, the faithful line up at the edge of the sanctuary platform and, having recited a brief profession of faith in the Real Presence, they, too, receive Holy Communion. Again we notice a remarkable departure from the Roman custom. Holy Communion is distributed to the laity by means of a small golden spoon. Instead of the round, familiar Host, the faithful are given a tiny portion of consecrated leavened bread, saturated with the Precious Blood. Immediately after Communion the congregation is blessed with the Holy Sacrament, another departure from the Roman Ritual. The ablution is completed not at the altar, but at the prothesis, since the Byzantines look upon the altar as the mystical Cross and consequently allow the performance there only of those acts which are intimately connected with the notion of sacrifice.

This, then, is the Liturgy according to the Byzantine ordinance. Undoubtedly, we seem to recognize some of the action in this ceremonial, but we are bewildered by the many differences between this service and that to which we are accustomed. "Can this be a Catholic church? And is this the unbloody Sacrifice of Christ?" Yes, the church we have visited is as Catholic as St. Patrick's Cathedral in New York or St. Peter's Basilica in Rome. The Liturgy we have attended is as Catholic as the Masses we hear in our local churches. And the clergymen and faithful we have seen and heard are as Catholic as our own parish priests and coparishioners. Like ourselves, they, too, profess the entire faith of Christ; they, too, have the seven sacraments instituted by Christ; they, too, are governed by their lawful pastors under the supreme direction of the Holy Father, the Pope of Rome.

"But then," we wonder, "why the dissimilar rites? Is there any purpose in perpetuating these strange customs in this land of the Latin Rite—where the Byzantine-Slavonic Rite is markedly in the minority?"

The problem cannot be fully appreciated without a knowledge of the turbulent history of the Rite. In the succeeding pages I will try to give a true picture of the historical background of the Christian Near East—so close and yet so far from the true center of Christianity. For the moment I wish to emphasize a point which should be everpresent in the minds of those who wish to work for the reunion of the separated Christian Near East with Rome.

The preachment of hatred against the Holy See and reunion have never been and are not today based upon doctrinal disagreements, as in the case with the Protestants. Today, as in the days of Cerularius, the theological disagreements concerning the Primacy of the Pope, the Procession of the Holy Spirit, the moment of Transubstantiation, Purgatory, and the Immaculate Conception, are only pretexts for this hostility; nor are they even often brought up, and the faith of the majority of the faithful is hardly at all affected by them.

The main—and highly effective—argument to which the anti-Catholic and antireunion propagandists always come back is one that touches the inmost heart of the Eastern people: the argument that the Holy See wishes to do away with their ancient rites and customs. In their understanding this means that the Holy See is bent on destroying their personality and individual nature. To illustrate this, let me quote the following from Catherine Zinsmayer in *The Chrysostom* (July, 1936):

When we compare the Roman Rite of the West with the rites of the Eastern Churches, some very interesting observations come to light. Since the liturgical rites are the outward expression of the inner soul of a Christian in union with God, the expression of what the mind conceives and the heart feels in its worship of God, the peculiar form which this expression assumes, reflects and is moulded by the character and genius of the people.

The character and the genius of the Romans in the West was one thing, that of the Eastern nations, another. The character of the people of the West is sometimes described as being largely extrovert, tending to outward activity, with a genius for law and order; cold, exact and precise in expression. The Roman Mass is a masterful expression of the people who form it . . . it is a thing of exquisite beauty, but cold and severe when compared to the Mass of the Eastern Rite. The character of the people of the East is quite different. They are by nature introvert, turning inward to the inner life of the soul, contemplative and rich in depth of emotion. To them the spiritual and the supernatural are so real that they seem almost to touch God Himself, and their hearts pour out their inner feeling in a never-ending variety of form and expression, inherited from the Greeks. They have built up a richness of ceremonial and symbolism in their liturgy which quite surpasses anything in the Latin rite.

This difference in character, permit me to stress again, should be remembered by all who sincerely desire to work for the great cause of the reunion of the separated East. In this regard I should like to point out an interesting fact. In countries ruled by the Dissidents many religious denominations were given freedom, or were at least tolerated, but invariably the Catholic Byzantine Rite was outlawed. Thus, for instance, in the nineteenth century, Imperial Russia granted religious freedom to the Catholics of the Latin Rite, but outlawed the Catholic Byzantine Rite. The same thing occurred in Greece. And even in some countries where the Rite was granted freedom, the politicians found ways and means to humiliate its members so that few entertained a desire to embrace it.

Why were these Catholics outlawed? Why were they humiliated? Because the enemies of the Church realized that a Catholic Church of the Byzantine Rite, flourishing in that country, would give the people a living proof that they are able to be Catholics and at the same time retain their rites and customs.

Let us return to the question: "Why perpetuate the Byzantine Rite? What good purpose, if any, can it serve?" The answer to this was contained in the words of Pope Urban VIII in a pronouncement directed to the Catholics of the Byzantine-Slavonic Rite: "In you I place my hope of converting the East." The Holy See does not regard the Byzantine Rite as an ancient relic or museum piece that must be coddled until it disintegrates. The Byzantine Rite has a great mission, it must not only be preserved; it must be developed and revitalized, so that in the fullness of time it may give the lie to the propaganda that poisoned the mind and heart of millions against the Holy See.

I have no doubt that it was Divine Providence that established the Byzantine Rite in this country where, far from the political intrigues of the Old World, it could regain its ancient splendor and vitality, where it could call out to our separated brethren and invite them back to their Father's home, there to continue worshipping according to their own customs, but with the added benefit of unity in faith and charity. This is the great mission of the Byzantine Rite; this is the great trust for which a handful of people has been valiantly fighting for centuries despite misunderstanding, persecution, and often martyrdom. And this great mission, the salvation of millions, can only be accomplished if all Catholics, clergy and laity of both rites, work hand in hand not only to preserve, but also to build up and revitalize the Byzantine Rite.

In conclusion let me quote from a letter sent me by an Irish Catholic friend of mine:

At the moment it is no doubt true, at least in the United States, that most Greek Catholics are more familiar with Latin customs than we are with theirs. I do not know why this is so, I only know that the reasons I have seen advanced as the cause of this seeming Latin aloofness (indifference, carelessness, pride, etc.) are fictitious. I have yet to see a Latin—and I have interested quite a few in attending your churches—who was not happy over the experience, and who did not express an earnest desire for further knowledge of his fellow Catholics of the Eastern Rites.

I suggest that some Sunday morning you kneel side by side with your brethren of the Byzantine-Slavonic Rite, and when you hear the priest raise his voice to the Almighty saying: "For peace of the world, for the welfare of the Holy Churches of God and the unity of all, let us pray to the Lord," you, too, can add your voice to the chorus of the congregation as it cries out: "*Hospodi pomiluj*"—"Lord have mercy."

II

UNITY IN DIVERSITY

NO one could foresee the far-reaching consequences of the decree of Constantine the Great, whereby the capital of the Roman Empire was moved from Rome to an insignificant provincial town on the Bosphorus, known locally as Byzantium. The presence of the Emperor's luxurious court with its intrigues, corruption, and wicked ambition changed the quiet community into a hotbed of iniquity—religious as well as social. Constantinople, no longer called Byzantium, proved to be a very good place for men who were garbed in the sacred vestments of the Church, but who had abandoned the humble spirit of Christ to adopt the ambitions of worldly courtiers. The comparatively insignificant Bishop of Byzantium suddenly became a central figure in Constantinople. An insidious war was started on the supernatural power and dignity of the Popes, and with the centuries a crack widened into a chasm, climaxed in 1054 by the disastrous break known as the great Greek Schism. The Popes, the divinely appointed guardians of humanity's spiritual welfare, never relaxed in their efforts to heal this wound inflicted on the Mystical Body of Christ. After many futile attempts, after sufferings and hardships, it seemed that God, moved at last by the pleas and tears of the Church, would restore its unity. In 1439, at the ecumenical council in Florence, the representatives of the East and West came to an understanding and with great joy the Church announced that once again unity reigned among Christians. This unity, however, did not last long; the enactments of the Council are remembered only as the generous but vain efforts of Rome to re-establish unity among Christians. The Council of Florence, nevertheless, is of great importance in the history of the Church, first, because it authoritatively defined the minimum requirements of Catholic unity; secondly, because it gave an incentive to more vigorous action for church unity, which later resulted in the return of many lost sheep, particularly of the millions of Ruthenians commonly known in this country as Greek Catholics.

Desiring to call the attention of humanity to these generous efforts of the Holy See—as well as to the benefits received by those people who, heeding the pleas of the Popes, entrusted their destinies into their hands—the late Pope

Pius XI ordered a world-wide celebration of this union proclaimed five hundred years ago.

While the satanic forces in Constantinople were preparing the final onslaught on the unity of the Church, Divine Providence was preparing for her a consolation. Intensive commercial relations with the Christian nations, efforts of lone Western missioners, as well as direct royal negotiations with the Court at Constantinople, finally resulted in the conversion of the heathen Slavonic tribes inhabiting the lands north of the Carpathian Mountains. The example set by their ruler St. Vladimir, who is said to have been baptized in 988, was followed by his subjects, and, one by one, the tribes paid their tribute to Christ and accepted His yoke in the sacrament of baptism in 989. Although in close contact with Constantinople, the original Christian Church in Russia was Catholic and acknowledged the Pope as its sovereign. As a matter of fact, Russia never officially notified Rome of her schism, but unfortunate circumstances in the thirteenth century, together with the ever growing influence of Constantinople (which persistently fostered ignorance and gave out misleading propaganda), slowly separated the Russian Church from Rome and led her through the schismatical portal of Constantinople. Thus the Russian Church started on the road of tragic adventure which ended with the horrors of the Russian revolution and atheistic Bolshevism.

Mindful of the great hopes of the Popes that a day shall dawn when Russia will return to the universal Father of mankind, His Holiness Pope Pius XII several years ago requested that all Catholics commemorate the anniversary of Russia's conversion to Christianity, praying that the Almighty would effect the second and permanent conversion of a great nation chastened by centuries of misfortune.

Again, in 1944, His Holiness wrote the Encyclical *Orientalis ecclesiae decus,* commemorating the fifteen-hundredth anniversary of the death of St. Cyril of Alexandria. Once more he urged the separated Eastern Churches to return to the faith of that great champion of the Catholic Church.

On December 23, 1946, Pope Pius XII issued the Encyclical *Orientales omnes,* commemorating the three-hundredth anniversary of the Union of Brest-Litovsk. Once again the Holy Father recounted the efforts of the Holy See to heal the great breach and enumerated some of the great spiritual, social, and cultural benefits received by those who heeded this plea. Briefly he told the little-known story of the glorious martyrdom suffered by the Ruthenians because of their loyalty to the Vicar of Christ and exhorted the persecuted spiritual descendants of those glorious martyrs to preserve until final victory. While it is true that "the present is dark and the future is uncertain and full of cares," this need not discourage us, for "the Lord keeps faith with us" (II Thess. 3:3).

Before we can undertake to do our share in this apostolate so dear to the heart of the Supreme Pontiff, we must have some knowledge of the events which shaped the destinies of the Eastern peoples during the long course of centuries, but, above all, of the principles which gave rise to a variety of rites in the unity of faith—a privilege exclusive to the Catholic Church.

Hence, before I begin sketching the history of the Slavs of the Byzantine Church, I will try to explain the principles that fostered the development of the various rites in the Catholic Church.

The earthly mission of our Lord can be looked upon as an effort to reunite all mankind into one great family, wherein God would be the universally acknowledged and worshipped Father, and every person—regardless of color, race, nation, sex, or social standing—would be a member of this divinely adopted family. This great mission, however, could not be achieved by natural principles of unity, since these principles have done nothing to prevent the present division of mankind. Racial and family ties, customs and languages, local circumstances, climate and culture, at one and the same time served as principles of union and division; consequently, they could not serve as a basis of the unity for which Christ was made man, for which He toiled, suffered and died, sealing it as the most sacred union between God and man with His own most precious blood. To effect this unity, and to insure its permanence, He built it on the supernatural principles of unity in faith, communion, and government. At the same time He endowed it with flexibility, with an elasticity whereby, no matter to what nations or under what local circumstances it should be applied, it would remain unchanged, yet retain whole the existing variety willed by the Creator Himself.

And thus Christ gave us the most beautiful thing in the world—a "continuously living miracle," to use the words of the Vatican Council. This miracle is a congregation of people from all over the world who profess the faith of Jesus Christ, partake of the same sacraments, and are governed by their lawful pastors under one visible head, the Pope—briefly, our Mother, the Holy Catholic Church, "where," as St. Paul says, "there is neither Gentile nor Jew, circumcision nor uncircumcision, Barbarian nor Scythian, bond nor free. But Christ is all, and in all" (Col. 3:11).

There can be no doubt that God founded the Synagogue—the Jewish unity. But, because this unity was to serve only one nation of one particular age, because it did not have a universal character and scope and was not intended to last until the end of time, certain rites of Jewish worship, though divinely-sanctioned, had in time to become obsolete.

On the Sabbath day (our Saturday) an Orthodox Jew living in a modern home will not strike a match to light a cigarette, will not touch the light switch, nor will he turn the knob of his automatic stove. If you ask him why not, he will tell you that such is the law of God. If you argue that God only prohibited menial labor on the Sabbath, he will show you that it is expressly stated (Exod. 35:3) that on the Sabbath no one is allowed to kindle fire, and there can be no doubt that striking a match, lighting his stove, or even turning on the electricity is "kindling fire." You might argue that the prohibition in Exodus had in view the kindling of fire as it was practiced in the days of Moses, that is, when it entailed long and strenuous labor, but the Orthodox Jew will not be impressed. Similar criticisms may be leveled at the numerous ceremonial laws ordained in the Old Testament: these served a well-defined and good purpose in the designs of God, but a limited one—one whose need passed with time.

When our Lord founded His Church, He envisioned not one nation in a certain age, but all mankind until the end of time, with its variety of customs, languages, and so forth. He avoided the sanctioning of legislation or institutions that might give rigidity to His Church, causing her to become obsolete or unreasonable. For this reason, Christ on the one hand was definite and inexorably firm in matters pertaining to the constitution of this unity, as well as in matters pertaining to faith, external communion and government, by which He insured the wondrous act of Divine Providence known to all as the world-wide and everlasting unity of the Catholic Church. But nowhere do we find Him prescribing detailed customs, actions, or devotions, similar to the ceremonial laws of the Old Testament. These matters He left to the Church, to the piety and prudence of His representatives and followers. Thus we find that Christ obliged all to be baptized in the name of the Father, Son and Holy Ghost; He did not say, however, whether this was to be done by aspersion, immersion, or ablution; nor did He specify (with the exception of the sacramental formula identical in all rites of the Church) the amount or form of prayer or material adjuncts to be used (for example, salt is used in the Latin, but not in the Oriental rites).

We find Christ ordering His Apostles to offer unto God the Father the sacrifice of bread and wine, repeating His own words of Consecration, but nowhere did He stipulate the time of day that this was to be done, nor does He say that the vestments are to be Byzantine, Gothic, or Roman. It was not the law of Jesus Christ nor of the Apostles that the

Consecration is to be preceded by the Introit, Collect, scriptural texts, Credo, Offertory, and Preface, as found in the Roman Mass; or the Antiphona, Trisagion, scriptural texts, litanies, Offertory, Credo and Anaphora, as found in the Byzantine Liturgy.

Our Lord gave a law, "Amen, amen I say unto you: Except you eat the flesh of the Son of man, and drink his blood, you shall not have life in you" (John 6:54), but He did not command that we do so once a year or every day of the year, nor does He tell us to receive His Body and Blood under one species—as Catholics of the Latin Rite do, or under both species—as Catholics of some Eastern Rites do.

From these examples, which may be indefinitely multiplied, it is evident that Christ had but one concern: that His Church maintain unity in matters of faith and morals, in communion of the sacraments, and in unity of ecclesiastical government. This triple unity ultimately resolves itself into communion with St. Peter and his legitimate successors, the Popes of Rome. Because of this solicitude, and because of Christ's command that His Apostles and their legitimate successors go to all the nations, even to the consummation of time, "teaching them to observe all things whatsoever I have commanded you" (Matt. 28:20), it is not only possible for the Catholic Church, but it is her exclusive privilege, to have more than a score of different rites, externally different, yet, in the fullest sense of the word, one and the same, and truly Catholic. This unity in diversity, an exclusive feature of the Catholic Church, is a miracle. By the will and the grace of her Founder, the Catholic Church has accomplished what in all other faiths has proved to be the impossible. By the unity of faith, communion, and government, she reunited the scattered nations of the world, but, while she reunited them and made them one, she also preserved their diversity, sanctified it, and gave her children a wide range of liberty wherein they could express their faith in accordance with their temperament, customs, and national traits.

Of the many parables told by our Lord in describing the nature and the growth of His Church, the parable of the tree is perhaps the most popular. Its generally accepted interpretation deals with the growth and ever increasing vitality of the Church. Yet, without any irreverence to the traditional interpretation, this parable might also be used to illustrate the following point.

A tree is influenced by its surroundings. The one and the same tree, retaining its essential characteristics, may, under certain climatic conditions, acquire certain peculiarities which it presents nowhere else. Thus, the so-called stone pine, in its native Southern Europe, reaches a height of from fifty to sixty feet, and has the shape of an enormous parasol; in England, however, it seldom exceeds the size of a large bush.

The Church of Christ is a tree which, by its very catholic (i.e., universal) nature, cannot be confined to a given locality. The Church is destined to spread to every land and grow in every land, serving all the peoples of all times. The first seed was sown in the homeland of the Chosen Race, but it has spread from there, and now there is hardly a nation or province in the world where it is not. As a pine tree remains a pine tree wherever it may grow, even though it assumes certain characteristics peculiar to the given locality, such as its foliage, stature, color, and shape, in like manner the Catholic Church remains the same forever in its essential nature; under the influence of the local circumstances of different nations, it, too, assumes certain accidental changes.

Aside from the three essential elements which make up the structure of the Church, there are other so-called secondary or accidental factors which enter into the structure of the Church. Such factors, for instance, are: the manner of worship and the manner of administering the sacraments; the language used in the liturgical services; the style, type, color, and number of vestments used by the clergy; the sacred vessels; the architecture of the church. Because these factors are only secondary and incidental to the structure of the Church, it is not necessary that they be the same for all nations.

Consequently, should we desire to find out whether or not a particular church is Catholic, we must ask three questions: Does that particular church profess the faith of Christ as proposed to our belief by the Catholic Church? Do its faithful partake of the sacraments administered by the Catholic Church? Is that church governed by a lawful pastor under the supreme direction of the successor of St. Peter, the Pope of Rome? If to all three questions the answer is Yes, we know that the church in question is Catholic, even though we may be confronted with certain religious practices totally strange to us.

Thus, if a church claims to be Catholic, it must have, to cite one instance, baptism; it is not necessary that the baptism be administered in the same manner, just so long as the form and matter instituted by Christ are observed. The Church had at one time or another three ways of administering baptism—by aspersion, by immersion, and by ablution. Were we to see someone baptizing by immersion, could we say they were not Catholics? A church which claims to be Catholic must have the Holy Eucharist and must distribute Holy Communion; her priests must be duly ordained ministers of Christ with power to consecrate and to change bread and wine into the Sacred Body and Precious Blood of Christ. But the ceremonies of the Holy Sacrifice need not necessarily be the same. Our Lord did command us to receive Holy Communion, but He did not tell us to do so in a kneeling posture, nor did He command us to receive Holy Communion in a standing posture and under both species. Would you have the right to say that a person receiving Holy Communion under both species in a standing posture was not a Catholic? Were we to walk into a church where the nave was separated from the sanctuary by a screen decorated with sacred paintings, could we say that that church was not a Catholic Church? Were we to meet a human being, would we fail to recognize it as a human being simply because it is not of our stature, color or race? On the other hand, if an ingenious sculptor managed to make a perfect wax replica of ourselves, would we look upon it as a human being?

Like the pine tree, the living Tree of Christ, the Catholic Church is not limited to one type. This divine Tree has many branches varying in size and shape; it has foliage of multiple hues. The Catholic Church is divided into the Church of the Latin Rite, the Byzantine Rite, the Maronite Rite, and several other rites. All this means is that in the Catholic Church one has the opportunity to worship God and be sanctified according to the ceremonies developed in the ancient ecclesiastical provinces of Rome, Byzantium, Antioch, and elsewhere.

Rite includes: first, all the ceremonies connected with the administration of the sacraments and particularly with the offering of the Holy Sacrifice; second, the series of psalms, lessons, prayers, etc., which make up the Divine Office; and third, all other religious and ecclesiastical functions known as sacramentals.

The Catholic Church has never maintained a principle of uniformity in rite. Just as there are different local laws in various parts of the Church, whereas certain fundamental laws are obeyed by all, so Catholics in different places have their local or national rites; they say prayers and perform ceremonies that have evolved to suit people of the various countries, and are only different expressions of the same fundamental truths. The essential elements of the functions are obviously the same everywhere and are observed by all Catholic rites in obedience to the command of Christ and the Apostles, . . . In the amplification of these essential elements in the accompanying prayers and the practical or symbolic ceremonies, various customs have produced the changes which make the different rites.[1]

[1] "Rites," *Catholic Encyclopedia,* XIII, 64.

The Church, in view of her many rites, may be seen as a garden containing flowers of various hues, various shapes, various fragrances; but when viewed as a whole, the Church forms one beautiful garden. Or, in the words of Pope Pius XI, the variety of the rites of the Catholic Church can be "likened unto a modulated harmony of voices rising from the earth to the Heavens."

Our Lord, then, left it up to His representatives and followers to prescribe the details of worship. This applies to the various Catholic rites taken as a whole, but it also applies to the constitution of a given rite. Thus, for example, during the Paschal Supper, obligatory under the Mosaic Law, our Lord took bread (leavened or unleavened, no one can say definitely) and wine and uttering the words of Consecration changed them into His Body and Blood.

Let us consider this scene. An ordinary room was the forerunner of our magnificent cathedrals, a plain dining table instead of our sumptuous altars, His humble clothing instead of our resplendent vestments, and He handed His disciples an ordinary cup that centuries later was replaced by vessels of untold value. The supper was opened and concluded by prescribed psalms, the conversation made up of the last instructions of the mortal Christ spoken in the Aramaic language. This is the true biblical picture of the first Mass celebrated by Christ, the founder of the Church.

Here we find no trace of our lengthy prayers, no indication of our ceremonies. Only a plain supper with some simple prayers—but a miraculous event taking place in a subdued, mysterious atmosphere. For many years later the Apostles, "remembering the salutary commandment and all things done for us" (Liturgy of St. John Chrysostom), continued to repeat the Mass, probably in the same manner. It was their piety and other factors of a more practical aspect that later inspired the Christians to surround this event, the greatest event in their daily life, as well as the administration of other sacraments, with certain symbols, preparations and precautions, lengthy prayers, and various signs of devotion. Being human and unable to forget the exigencies of the flesh, the Christians needed visible, tangible, material symbols by which they could give vent to their religious aspirations. And because they realized that all that is best and noblest must be made subservient to the worship of the Lord and Creator, the Christians applied themselves to making the services of God beautiful. In doing this they wished also to impress the pomp of the worship of God upon the minds and imaginations of men.

As the Church, in the passing centuries, carried the simple Sacrifice of Christ to more and more nations and tribes, many of these tried to beautify it and adorn it with such symbols and prayers as best suited their temperament and their local circumstances. In a relatively short time the Christians, scattered throughout the Roman Empire, had evolved a great variety of symbols and prayers for the beautifying of the one and only Sacrifice of God. The symbols and prayers varied with every large community, and, with abuses beginning to crop up, greater unity in this matter was seen to be needed. With the final victory of the Church in the fourth century, the liturgy went through a period of reorganization.

In the early Church people were divided into Patriarchates according to the geographical position of their races. At first there were diversities of local rites and customs in each country, almost in each diocese or local church. Then gradually, almost insensibly, came the ideal of uniformity throughout each Patriarchate. *This is merely one special case of the general centralization, not so far under one chief Patriarch at Rome (that is another matter), but under each Patriarch within his own Patriarchate. As each priest would naturally follow the rite of his Bishop, so each Bishop followed that of his Metropolitan, and each Metropolitan that of his Patriarch. . . .*

Each diocese adopted the rite of its Patriarchal city. The rite used by any Bishop became a kind of symbol of his dependence on a certain Patriarch. . . .

Thus the Christians of Egypt obeyed the Patriarch of Alex-

andria and used the Alexandrine rite; those of Syria obeyed him of Antioch and used his rite and so on.[1]

Thus we find the Church developing five great liturgical families—in the East, the liturgies of Jerusalem and Antioch, the liturgies of Mesopotamia and Persia, the liturgies of Egypt and finally that of Byzantium; in the West, the various liturgies under the Patriarch of Rome. Thus it happened that Christians in Jerusalem, Alexandria, Antioch, Constantinople, and Rome offered the same Sacrifice, but in those different places this one Sacrifice was adorned with prayers and symbols corresponding to the temperament of people, who as Christians were one, but as men were members of different nations. Thus the Catholic Church accomplished the impossible: she maintained her unity but also retained the diversity of her children; she forged them into one body, but let them do their work as they best saw fit.

In this, the Catholic Church can be compared to the working of the human mind, for as a linguist can express the same thought in many languages without destroying its identity, so the Catholic Church can profess the same faith, can have the same communion and the same government through the various rites she inspired and sanctified

[1] Adrian Fortescue, *The Uniate Eastern Church* (London, Burns, Oates & Washbourne, Ltd., 1923), 12.

by the grace of her immortal Spouse, our Lord Jesus Christ.

It is most difficult to describe adequately the beauty of the Church in the variety of her rites. At a loss for words, Pope Pius XI adopted the inspired words of David and in his encyclical letter *Ecclesia Dei* spoke of the Church as a "Queen . . . in gilded clothing, surrounded with variety" (Ps. 44:10). As once the queen of Sheba emerged from the desert wastes to bring homage and gifts to Solomon, so the Church emerges from the wastes of this valley of tears to adore and glorify her Spouse, Master, and King, Jesus Christ. Whether she be adorned in the glittering gown stitched by the intricate symbolism of the mystical East, or clad in the plain garment woven by the practical West, she remains the Spouse of her divine Master and the Mother of redeemed mankind. She repeats the inspired words of the Apostle of the Gentiles: "There is no distinction of the Jew and the Greek: for the same is Lord over all, rich unto all that call upon him" (Rom. 10:12), and she directs her Children in the East to pray with St. John Chrysostom: "Praying to our Lord for unity of all," that, "taking into consideration the faithful of His Church, He may deign to bring peace and unity according to His holy Will."

Commenting upon the *Kyrie,* an Eastern invocation widely used by East and West, Maurice Zundel keenly observes[2] that the survival of this Greek invocation in the Roman liturgy is due, not to chance, but to Divine Providence.

East and West still find themselves in inimical camps. The profound tragedy of the situation is that the real issues in this dispute were settled centuries ago by third parties. All that remains now is for East and West to exchange the kiss of peace. East and West constantly use the *Kyrie,* a simple but profound invocation, which, if properly understood, should remind us all to seek, not personal interests, but what is desired by Christ, unity.

It is true, we cannot by-pass the real theological questions which separate us, nor can we demand that the Church of Rome be "unfaithful to the witness she never ceased to bear to Christ, as the living teacher in the person of Peter and his successors." Nevertheless, overemphasis on existing differences and meticulous concern with subordinate aspects of controversies that embitter existing differences will only broaden the cleavage.

The *Kyrie,* repeated daily in the East and the West, is one outstanding symbol of the main points of essential agreement between the two separated bodies of Christians. Through the understanding of this essential agreement and

[2] *The Splendor of the Liturgy* (New York, 1939), 46-48.

the skillful application of St. Augustine's axiom, "Unity in things necessary, liberty in accidentals, but charity in all things," the Fathers at the Council of Florence found a way to bridge the gap of schism caused centuries ago by a language which failed to express the riches and true contents of this essential agreement. In any case, holiness itself will be the most powerful means of a reunion of all Christians.

III

THE BYZANTINE RITE

THE two essential factors that constitute our Catholic worship—the matter and form of the sacraments and of the Holy Sacrifice, which were instituted by our Lord and which no human power can change—have been explained. Other factors which surround the divinely established essential elements are the so-called accidental ones, and are of human origin. These accidental factors may vary. Their variety is not only permissable, but even desirable, so long as they are not contrary to the essential elements.

The same human thought may be expressed in many languages and, so long as the thought or idea is not perverted, no one will reasonably object to the use of different words. Similarly, when people adopted the Catholic religion, which was and is intended to be a universal religion, they accepted the essential elements of Christian means of sanctification, but surrounded these elements with external signs of piety, gratitude, and sanctity, such as prayers and other ceremonies. These external signs were executed according to the taste, the temperament, the customs, and the local necessities of those who adopted Catholicism.

As a result of the divine unity and flexibility of Catholic worship, the Catholic Church has developed more than a score of rites, fundamentally the same, yet varying considerably in detail of ceremonial.

All liturgies of the various rites in the Catholic Church follow the same pattern and consist of two principal parts. The first is the Mass of the catechumens; the other the Mass of the faithful. The Mass of the catechumens is a Christian adaptation of the synagogue's official daily service, which consisted in the singing of psalms or other hymns, readings from Holy Writ, and an explanation of scriptural passages. To these the Christians added the reading of prayers for the catechumens preparing for baptism. On the other hand, the Mass of the faithful, strictly Christian, consisted of the Preface or Anaphora, the Sacrifice (Transubstantiation), the Lord's Prayer, Communion, and thanksgiving for favors received.

This sequence of religious acts is patterned on the Last Supper; it constitutes the Eucharistic Sacrifice exactly as practiced by the Apostles and their disciples. It is the general order of prayers and ceremonies in every known liturgy in the Church. Psalms and hymns (called the Introit or Antiphona); readings from the Scriptures, with a sermon and prayers for the prospective faithful; the Great Thanksgiving (Preface or Anaphora); the Consecration, the Mementos, the Lord's Prayer, Holy Communion, and conclusion of the Liturgy.

It was from this skeleton that the Church developed a variety of ceremonials, which gave birth to the various rites now existing.

There are four parent rites from which all other rites derive. These are: The Antiochene, the Alexandrine, the Roman, and the Gallican, the last of which no longer exists. This book deals primarily with the Antiochene liturgy.

The Antiochene and the Alexandrine liturgies are the oldest. The Alexandrine liturgy had its origin in Egypt and neighboring regions. The Antiochene liturgy was used throughout Asia Minor, particularly in Syria and Palestine. When the missionaries from the churches subordinated to the Patriarch in Antioch were sent out to convert other nations, these converts adopted the ritual of the Church of Antioch, and added local color to it. When the see of Byzantium was established, it, too, adopted the ritual of Antioch. It was in Byzantium that the ancient rite of Antioch underwent a change and became what is now known as the Byzantine (or Greek) Rite.

The Byzantine Rite, which, after the Roman Rite, has the largest number of adherents, has three liturgies. The founding of the first is attributed to the great Father of the Church, St. Basil, Archbishop of Caesarea in Cappadocia; another is attributed to St. John Chrysostom, Archbishop of Constantinople; the third, attributed to Pope Gregory the Great, the Liturgy of the Presanctified Gifts, is celebrated during Lent.

It must be remembered that all living rites are subject to gradual modification. The structure and essential characteristics of the rite remain the same, yet new prayers and new ceremonies are fitted into it. This is precisely what happened to the Antiochene Rite in Cappadocia. The fundamental Antiochene type remained, but was augmented by various local customs and prayers composed by the local clergy. In some places, therefore, the liturgy became quite lengthy, sometimes lasting several hours.

Proclus of Constantinople, a biographer of St. Basil the Great, has this to say concerning the liturgy then in use: "When the great Basil saw the carelessness and degeneracy of men who feared the length of the liturgy—not as if he himself thought it too long—he shortened its form, so as to remove the weariness of the clergy and assistants." To this reform, St. Basil added others. He introduced a new manner of chanting psalms; he eradicated many abuses and introduced elements which harmonized with the need of his day and with the dignity of Christian worship. The authority and fame of St. Basil made possible the acceptance of his reforms, and, two years after his death, St. Gregory of Nazianzus, called to administer the Church in Constantinople (in 381), found the liturgy there almost identical to that in use in Cappadocia. This liturgy revised by St. Basil is considered the first Byzantine liturgy.

A few years later, another great Father of the Church, St. John Chrysostom, Patriarch of Constantinople, was confronted with the same problems that had moved St. Basil to revise the liturgy. Amid the worldliness and dissipation of the imperial city many abuses crept into the liturgy; many complained about the length of St. Basil's liturgy and for this reason did not attend divine services. Following the example of St. Basil, St. John Chrysostom revised the liturgy.

On the basis of the references to the liturgy made by St. John in his homilies, liturgical experts have attempted to reconstruct the liturgy as it was in his day. The service began with the bishop's greeting, followed by lessons from the Prophets and Apostles. The deacon read the Gospel; after the Gospel the bishop preached. At the conclusion of the sermon the bishop prayed over the catechumens and the faithful. This was followed by the Kiss of Peace, the Eucharistic prayer, Consecration, the intercession with the memory of the saints, the mementos for the dead and the living, a short litany, the Lord's Prayer, Holy Communion, and a prayer of thanksgiving. Holy Communion was received under both species. In St. John's time it seems that the faithful received both species separately, drinking from the chalice.

Since this order of the liturgy was reconstructed from the writings of the saint, authorities concluded that the liturgy of St. John Chrysostom was in great part written in Antioch, and that he introduced it at Constantinople when he became patriarch.

Those familiar with the modern version of St. John's liturgy, as used today in the Byzantine Rite by Catholics as well as by Orthodox, will notice the absence in the reconstructed liturgy of the long, multiple litanies, the Preparation of the Offering (Proskomedia), the Little Entrance before the Gospel, the Cherubic Hymn, the Great Entrance in its present form, and the Creed. All these elements were added to St. John's liturgy during the succeeding centuries, until it lost its original brevity.

Byzantium had been an insignificant provincial town. Its bishop was a suffragan of Heraclea in Thrace (European Turkey) and as such used the liturgy of Antioch. In the year 324, Emperor Constantine the Great decided to move the capital of the Roman Empire from Rome to Byzantium on the Bosphorus. The small but beautiful town was renamed Constantinople, i.e., the city of Constantine, and on May 11, 330, it was solemnly dedicated as the new capital of the Empire.

With the presence of the imperial court the significance and influence of the local bishop grew by leaps and bounds. Finally, the Second Ecumenical Council, convoked in 381, separated the Byzantine suffragan see from the metropolitan authority of Heraclea and, disregarding the rights of Antioch and Alexandria, gave the Bishop of Constantinople the patriarchal title and the first place in honor and dignity after the Bishop of Rome. After this, the Bishop of Constantinople claimed and exercised jurisdiction over the six ecclesiastical provinces of Thrace, hitherto subject to Heraclea. Soon afterwards, he extended his jurisdiction over the entire territory of Asia Minor and Pontus, a long and narrow strip of land along the southern coast of the Black Sea, which had twenty-two ecclesiastical provinces previously subject to the metropolitan sees of Ephesus and Caesarea. This was an obvious usurpation of rights. Yet it was sanctioned by the twenty-eight canons of the Council of Chalcedon, held in 431, and as a result Constatinople ruled over 420 dioceses. This usurpation of rights, together with the claims of primacy advanced by the Bishop of Constantinople at this time, was at the bottom of the long conflict between Constantinople and Rome which culminated in the Eastern Schism of 1054. In 733 the province of Illyricum, with more than one hundred dioceses hitherto subject to the Pope, was by imperial edict withdrawn from the jurisdiction of the Bishop of Rome. In this manner, toward the end of the ninth century, Constantinople exercised jurisdiction over 624 dioceses, composed of 51 metropolitan sees, 51 exempt archbishoprics, and 522 suffragan bishoprics. Geographically, this covered the Balkans, European Turkey, and most of Asia Minor.

This enormous jurisdictional aggrandizement brought with it important liturgical changes at the expense of the other ancient rites in the East.

In those days the emperors wielded great power and influence in the Church. They took an active part in the liturgy, particularly at the Offertory. As a natural consequence, the ceremonies of the ancient ritual of Antioch were revised and supplemented in a manner to fit the majesty of emperors, who reveled in the lavish splendor of Oriental ceremonies. These rites, originally intended for state occasions only, became common practice. Thus, the so-called Little and Great Entrances in the Byzantine liturgy are but pale shadows of the great imperial processions.

Ecclesiastical provinces, subject to the jurisdiction of Constantinople, needed little urging to accept these lavish rites, which appealed to their imagination and aesthetic sense. In other instances, where efforts were made to reject the jurisdiction and liturgy of Constantinople, the emperors and patriarchs suppressed the ancient rituals of other patriarchal sees.

The average Catholic, as well as non-Catholic, is of the opinion that Rome forcibly imposed her rites and customs on the peoples her missionaries converted to the Church, and that Constantinople, inspired probably by greater charity, held fast to the ancient traditions and allowed its subjects freedom in choosing and developing their rites. The facts, however, are different. Rome allowed the nations converted by and subject to her jurisdiction to insert into her traditional rites and customs some of their own; Constantinople, on the other hand, suppressed all other rites and imposed upon their adherents the observance of its own rites, going to the extent of refusing to sanction even some of the oldest and most hallowed traditions of the East. Thus, for instance, the use of the Slavonic language in the liturgy was suppressed in Bulgaria and replaced with Greek. The Georgians, one of the oldest Christian peoples, suffered much from Constantinople and, when they found themselves under Russian rule, they were forced to give up the use of their own language, customs and rites and to adopt the Slavonic version of the Byzantine liturgy. In like manner, many of the ancient Eastern customs were suppressed. The ancient custom of Jerusalem—the renewal of the Easter fire—still observed in the Latin Rite—is no longer known to the Byzantine Rite; the feast of the Exaltation of the Holy Cross, once a holy day celebrated with splendor rivaling Easter Sunday, has now become, in the Byzantine Rite, a day of mourning with the obligation to keep a "black fast."

In this manner, the liturgies attributed to St. Basil and St. John Chrysostom, together with the "Presanctified" liturgy of St. Gregory, became a common heritage of the Orthodox East, while the other Eastern rites, with the exception of the Maronite Rite, managed to survive solely because they were used by the Eastern heretical churches which had nothing in common with Constantinople. This is the case of the Nestorians, Chaldeans, Malabars, Melankarese, Copts, and Ethiopians.

On the whole, an estimated 160 million people use the Byzantine liturgy in several languages, of which approximately eight million are Catholic. The Byzantine-Slavonic ritual used at the present time, except for changes in the language, was developed in the thirteenth and fourteenth centuries.

The Liturgy of St. Basil is celebrated on ten occasions in the year: on the eves of Christmas and Epiphany, on the feast day of St. Basil (January 1), on the first five Sundays in Lent, on Holy Thursday and on Holy Saturday. During Lent, from Monday through Friday, the Liturgy of the Presanctified Gifts is celebrated. On all other days the Liturgy of St. John Chrysostom is celebrated. The sole difference between the liturgies of St. Basil and St. John Chrysostom is that the former contains much longer prayers and thus takes longer to celebrate.

The Byzantine liturgy was translated into the languages of the people who have taken it for their own. Besides the original Greek, it is used in the Arabic, Georgian, Slavonic, and Rumanian languages. The Hungarian Catholics use an unauthorized Hungarian version. Among the Dissidents, the Esthonians, Letts, Germans, Finns, Tartars, Chinese, Japanese, Syrians, Albanians, and the natives of the Aleutian Islands use this liturgy. An attempt was made to introduce an American version of the liturgy for the benefit of the Dissidents in America. The movement has failed.

Of these groups the most important, so far as number and influence are concerned, is the Byzantine-Slavonic group. Of the eight million Eastern Catholics, six million belong to this rite. Of the 160 million Dissidents, approximately 125 million Slav Dissidents follow the Byzantine-Slavonic Rite.

IV

THE BYZANTINE-SLAVONIC VERSION

GOD, in His infinite goodness and in fulfillment of His divine promise that the gates of Hell would not prevail against His Church, had so directed the destinies of the Catholic Church that, whenever she suffered some temporary losses in one part of the world, she was compensated by new and abundant gains in another. Thus, the Reformation deprived the Church of millions of souls in Europe and the British Isles, but those losses were compensated by the opening of new and fruitful mission fields in China, India, and in the newly discovered Americas.

Likewise, when the evil forces brought about the Eastern Schism, consummated in 1054 by the Patriarch Cerularius, Divine Providence was preparing a new missionary harvest among the numerous tribes of the Slavs in Central and Eastern Europe.

Upon the ruins of the ancient Roman Empire, Charlemagne had established the new Frankish Empire which embraced northern Spain, France, Germany, northern Italy, and parts of Denmark. At about the same time in the East, the Byzantine Empire, ruled by the Roman Emperor, reached the height of its glory and power. Between these two great Christian empires lay the lands inhabited by pagan Slav tribes. The Slavs occupied the lands of the Balkans, as well as the whole of Central Europe and practically the entire continent of Europe east of the Oder River. It was here that the Byzantine-Slavonic Rite was born and developed.

The Slavs were a peaceful race. They expanded, not because of lust for conquest, but because of their ever increasing number. They were not a united people guided by powerful rulers. They led a tribal life and were governed by princes of varying and often modest power.

War and subjugation came to the Slavs through the assaults of Charlemagne, who penetrated the ancient province of Carinthia and the coastal regions of Dalmatia, and subjugated the Croats and the Slovenes. The Czechs peacefully held what is now Bohemia, and the Slovaks were settled on the fertile lands of Pannonia, present-day Hungary, and on the western slopes of the Carpathian Mountains and Moravia. At the close of the eighth century, the Franks penetrated the possessions of the Slovaks, around Lake Blatno, where they settled as peaceful colonists. The Austrian Bishops of Salzburg and Passau claimed these Slovak lands as parts of their diocesan jurisdiction, while the Bishop of Ratisbonne claimed jurisdiction over Bohemia.

The first to realize the political danger of this peaceful penetration of the Franks was the Slovak leader, Mojmir I, who set out to expel the Franks. To achieve his purpose he created a central state by rallying the lesser princes under one banner. His first act was to remove Pribina, the powerful prince of Nitra, but Pribina turned for aid to the German Emperor (Ludwig the Pious), and received the territory between the Danube and Drava Rivers to hold in fief. Pribina urged his people to become Christians and in Nitra he erected the first Christian church.

Meanwhile Mojmir clashed with the Franks and suffered defeat. His son, Rostislav, was placed at the head of the Moravian-Slovak state and ruled as a puppet for the Emperor. Rostislav consolidated his new state and concentrated all his efforts on freeing his country from Frankish domination. Finally, matters between Rostislav and the Emperor Ludwig came to a head in 855, and in the ensuing battle Rostislav defeated the Emperor's armies. The great Moravian state was formed.

Rostislav turned his attention to settling the internal problems of the new kingdom, foremost among which was the question of religion. When the Slavs first came into contact with Christianity through the Frankish colonists, this religion left little if any impression upon them. Rostislav favored Christianity and wished his people to adopt it, so he turned to the Emperor in Constantinople with the request that missionaries, fully acquainted with the Slavonic tongue, be sent to his land to preach Christianity. He reaped two personal gains from this action: he freed himself from the political influence of the Franks, and at the same time secured for himself a powerful political ally and protector against any possible Frankish militaristic move.

When Rostislav made his request to the Byzantine Emperor, the Church in Constantinople had a great and saintly missionary who had just returned from a missionary tour in Crimea. He was the renowned philosopher Constantine, or St. Cyril as we know him today, son of a Greek nobleman. He had a perfect knowledge of the Slavonic tongue. His great erudition, powerful oratory, and sanctity of life made him the logical choice of the Emperor for the Slavonic mission. Constantine was summoned to the imperial court, and, at Rostislav's request, he was instructed to leave immediately for Moravia in the company of his brother, Methodius.

Before leaving on their proposed journey, Cyril worked out an alphabet to express Slavonic sounds and made preparations to translate the liturgical and ecclesiastical books into Slavonic. A simplified form of this alphabet is known to this day as the Cyrillic alphabet.

Upon their arrival in Moravia in 863, these saintly brothers began the great task of translating the Byzantine liturgical books from the original Greek into the Slavonic language.[1] They gathered about themselves a group of disciples to aid them in the preaching of the Gospel. But their mission from the very start met with fierce opposition.

The Frankish clergy, who considered Moravia their ecclesiastical province, looked upon these missionaries from the East as intruders and usurpers. Moreover, the missionaries not only preached, but also offered the Holy Sacrifice, in a vernacular language—a thing unheard of in the West and, in the eyes of the Frankish clergy, a "sacrilege." Furthermore, the arrival and missionary activities of Cyril and Methodius coincided with the time when Pope Nicholas I excommunicated Photius for usurping the patriarchal see of Constantinople. This fact gave the Franks some ground to suspect the saintly brothers.

The Frankish bishops appealed to Rome and the brothers were summoned to the Eternal City. Cyril and Methodius appeared before Pope Adrian II and a synod of bishops, where they were forced to defend themselves against the

[1] This is the traditional opinion on this matter. Today, however, many authoritative scholars are inclined to believe that Sts. Cyril and Methodius translated the Roman Ritual into the Slavonic tongue.

accusations of the Frankish clergy. They proved that the use of the vernacular in the liturgy was an approved custom in the East and that by its use they were more successful in evangelizing the Slavs, at the same time preserving for them their independence from the Franks. The Pope and the synod approved. The Pope accepted the Slavonic liturgical books from the brothers, had them placed upon the altar of the cathedral church of Rome, St. Mary Major, and celebrated the divine Liturgy over them. In further confirmation of pontifical approval of the Slavonic liturgy, the Pope himself consecrated Cyril and Methodius as bishops. These events mark the official birth of the Slavonic version of the Byzantine liturgy.

While still in Rome, St. Cyril died in a Benedictine monastery. After the burial of his saintly brother, Methodius returned to Moravia as the archbishop of the re-established archdiocese of Sirmium, which included the lands of Moravia-Pannonia (prewar Czechoslovakia, Hungary, and part of Yugoslavia). With renewed zeal he set about converting the Slavs. The conversion of the Slovaks was virtually completed during his lifetime. He and his disciples also preached in Bohemia, but with little success; it was not till after the death of Methodius that Christianity began to take root among the Czechs. Poland is also said to have received the first seeds of Christianity from Methodius, and tradition has it that he founded the episcopal see of Lemberg. Pope Leo XIII mentions that Cyril was in Kiev (Russia), between 858 and 861. It is believed that while in Russia he taught the Russians the Slavonic alphabet and gave them liturgical books and a Slavonic translation of the Scriptures.

The victory of Methodius over his enemies did not end his trials nor those of the Byzantine-Slavonic Rite. The Bishops of Salzburg and Passau were angered, because Methodius had received part of their dioceses for his new archdiocese. Aided by the Frankish king, Ludwig, they set out to force his removal. They failed to halt the activities of Methodius and decided to resort to force. Methodius was summoned to Ratisbonne in 871, where the Frankish king and a synod of Frankish bishops deposed him and condemned him to prison. He was held in captivity for two and a half years. Finally, when Pope John VIII learned about the plight of Methodius, he threatened to excommunicate the Frankish bishops if he were not released. In 873, Methodius was permitted to return to his missionary work. Several years later a Benedictine named Wiching, upon the nomination of the Moravian king, Svyatopolk, was consecrated one of Methodius' suffragans as Bishop of Nitra. He renewed the attack upon Methodius and produced spurious Papal letters purporting to show that even Rome condemned Methodius and his Slavonic liturgy.

The controversy was finally brought to a head in 880 when Pope John VIII summoned Methodius to Rome for an investigation. A synod examined the charges and found him innocent. The Slavonic liturgy was sanctioned once more and the faithful of the Moravian Empire were ordered to respect and obey Methodius in all matters. In his message to Svyatopolk the Pontiff wrote:

We rightly praise the Slavonic letters invented by Cyril, in which praises to God are set forth, and we order that the glories and the deeds of Christ our Lord be told in that language. Nor is it in any wise opposed to wholesome doctrine and faith to celebrate Mass in that same Slavonic language, or to chant the Holy Gospel or divine lessons from the Old and New Testaments duly translated and interpreted therein, or the other parts of the Divine Office; for He who created the three principal languages, Hebrew, Greek and Latin, also made the others for His praise and glory.

This was the last trial Methodius had to face. About this time, he received an invitation from the Emperor of Constantinople to pay him a visit. Methodius hastened in the hope that he would be able to persuade the Emperor to heal the schism created by Photius. During his stay in Constantinople he went into seclusion with two other priests and they completed, with the exception of the Books of the Machabees, the Slavonic translation of the Scriptures, as well as the Nomocanon—the Greek ecclesiastical-civil code of laws.

Methodius returned to Moravia, where he died on April 6, 885. His passing marked the death of the Slavonic liturgy in western and central Europe. Wiching forcibly introduced the Latin Rite into Moravia and had the disciples of the apostle cast into prison and later banished from the country. These disciples carried the Slavonic liturgy to the Balkans. From there it was taken to Russia to be preserved by them and their descendants up to the present day.

While speaking of the saintly apostles of the Slavs, it will not be amiss to call attention to some inaccurate notions that prevail concerning the translation of the liturgy into the Slavonic language.

According to a statement made in the so-called Pannonian life of the Sts. Cyril and Methodius, the idea of translating the Byzantine liturgy into the Slavonic language was not conceived by St. Cyril. On the contrary, it was initiated by the Moravians themselves. These Moravians, so this legend tells us, had been Christianized by Latin missionaries, but they could not reconcile themselves to the fact that the worship was conducted in the Latin language. They knew that Constantinople was championing the use of the vernacular in the liturgy, hence, they turned to the Patriarch in Constantinople with the request that he give them a liturgy in their own language. The Patriarch, according to this legend, readily agreed to the request and commissioned St. Cyril to accomplish the task. This is what all Dissident Slavs believe about the origin of the Slavonic version of the Byzantine liturgy.

The intention to belittle the Latin West and arouse gratitude toward the Patriarch of Constantinople is so obvious that one cannot help but feel suspicious. As a matter of fact, Dr. Golubinsky, Russia's foremost authority on ecclesiastical history and a Dissident himself, submitted the whole matter to close scrutiny and did not hesitate to brand it as a legend.

First, it is difficult to conceive that a newly converted people should know about the possible use of the vernacular in the liturgy, particularly since at that time Constantinople was making every effort to suppress its use. Furthermore, although individual conversions among the Moravians did take place, the mass of the people were not converted until Sts. Cyril and Methodius undertook their mission. Therefore, one cannot speak of an established church among the Moravians until after the arrival of the two saintly brothers.

As already stated, the conversion of the Moravians resulted from a political and military alliance which, according to the custom of the period, entailed the acceptance of the religion of the more powerful ally. The Moravians were beginning to unite into one solid kingdom and showed signs of great power. To thwart any designs that the Moravians may have entertained against his empire, the Frankish Emperor entered into a military alliance with Bulgaria, a nation bordering on the south and southeast of the Moravians. To neutralize the danger presented by these Frankish allies to the south, Moravia entered into a political and military alliance with the powerful Emperor of Constantinople and, in return for military assistance, promised to accept Christianity as practiced in Constantinople. It was understood of course that the Gospel would be given to the people by Greek missionaries sent to them by Constantinople. Not a word was said about the Slavonic language or a Slavonic liturgy. Providence took a hand in the matter, and, St. Cyril, well versed in the Bulgarian language, was elected to head the Moravian mission. It was St. Cyril, and not the Patriarch, who was inspired by the idea of a liturgy in the vernacular.

Thus, the origin of the Slavonic version of the Byzantine liturgy was entirely due to the inspired initiative of St. Cyril, and can be considered as an attempt to break with the nationalistic policy of Constantinople in favor of an ancient ecclesiastical tradition forcibly suppressed by that patriarchal see. In support of his claim that this innovation was entirely due to the personal initiative of St. Cyril, Dr. Golubinsky calls attention to a number of writings of that period, preserved in unpublished manuscripts, in which several men defend the work of St. Cyril against the objections, invectives, and condemnations of Greek ecclesiastics.

The false legend, which is widely taken for the truth, should be a reminder to us of the crying need of accurate information in matters pertaining to the East. It accounts for many of the prejudices the Dissident peoples nurture toward the Catholic Church, and shows what a great amount of good will shall be needed before a successful mission can be started among them.

One other matter connected with the Slavonic language used in the liturgy should be cleared up.

The average person is under the impression that the language used in the Slavonic liturgy today is the parent tongue of the Slavic languages, as Latin is the parent tongue of the Romance languages. This is not so. At the time St. Cyril began translating the Byzantine liturgy into the Slavonic language, he undoubtedly made use of the vernacular language of the Moravians, a language quite distinct from the other Slavonic languages. When the rite was suppressed in Moravia and was later confined to the territorial limits of Bulgaria, the Bulgarians did not hesitate to revise the language to suit their people. This Moravo-Bulgarian version of the Byzantine liturgy was then passed on to the Russians and Serbians where it underwent a limited revision, confined mostly to grammatical changes. Hence, it is not true that the language used in the Byzantine liturgy is the Old Slavonic tongue. It is one of the languages used by the ancient Slavs—a Moravo-Bulgarian version slightly changed under the influence of the Russian grammar of the seventeenth and eighteenth centuries. Thus, when speaking of this language, it would appear to be more accurate to speak not of the Old-Slavonic, but of the Church-Slavonic language.

V

FLIGHT OVER THE SLAVONIC EAST

A STUDY of the history of the Byzantine-Slavonic Church will reveal that its curse and nemesis was political intrigue. One can conclude that the liberation and revival of her glory is predicated on her ability to cast off this ancient political curse.

The saintly brothers and apostles of the Slavs, Cyril and Methodius, generously offered their services and talents to the evangelizing of the Slavic races. Inspired by the custom of the East, where the vernacular was always adopted as the liturgical language, they believed that their mission among the Slavs would be more successful if they offered them the consolations of the Gospel in their native tongue, rather than in a language beyond their understanding. Consequently, when the saints came to evangelize the people of the then great and powerful Slav kingdom of Moravia, their first care was to work out an alphabet that would enable them to render the Gospel and all liturgical books used in the Byzantine Rite in a language familiar to the Moravians. Thus originated the Cyrillic alphabet and the Slavonic translation of the Scriptures and the Greek liturgy. Such, too, was the humble beginning of the Byzantine-Slavonic Rite.

Even then, political interests, whose machinations form the background of the rite's history, were intent on destroying it. The political might of Moravia was too great to suit the Frankish rulers. With the success of Sts. Cyril and Methodius and their aides, the influence of the Frankish interests were diminishing. Hence the Frankish bishops, probably under pressure from their rulers, denounced the work of the saints and had them deposed and imprisoned as heretics and schismatics. Even after Pope John VIII solemnly confirmed their work and established the archbishopric in Moravia, political pressure still continued. The death of Methodius was followed shortly by the disintegration of the Moravian kingdom, and finally the Byzantine-Slavonic Rite was discontinued in Western Europe. This was the first triumph of corrupt politics. For many centuries after, the Byzantine-Slavonic Rite was confined exclusively to the Eastern Slavs.

Of the many Slavonic races inhabiting the continent of

Europe today, the following have adopted and kept the Slavonic version of the Byzantine Rite: Bulgarians, Yugoslavians—with the exception of the majority of the Croatians and Slovenes—the various Slavs inhabiting the former empire of Russia, Ukrainians, and the Rusinians of Carpatho-Russia. Of these the Bulgarians, Russians and Ruthenians played the most important part in history, and they will be the subject of our discussion.

The Bulgarians originally were Turanians who had invaded the northern provinces of the Byzantine Empire from Central Asia, and finally settled in Illyricum. Here they came into contact with and mingled with the Slavs adopting their language and customs. They became the greatest factor in the dispute between Rome and Constantinople.

The Bulgarians were converted to Christianity by Constantinople in 865 during the reign of Prince Bogoris, but the Patriarch neglected to establish a hierarchy. As a result, abuse involving false priests and imposters was rampant. Desiring to stop this, Prince Bogoris turned to Pope St. Nicholas I with the request that a patriarchate be established. The Pope turned down the request; instead he established an archbishopric at Achrida. This action of the Holy See provoked bitterness in Constantinople. The Bulgars had settled in Illyricum, which covered the territories known today as Bosnia, Serbia, European Turkey, Greece and Crete, over which the Popes had claimed immediate jurisdiction since Apostolic days. On the other hand the Byzantine emperors by their own laws claimed it for themselves. Here again, we are confronted with the specter of intriguing politics.

A claim is made that Rome declared the Archbishop of Achrida a Patriarch in 924 and that he was recognized as such by Constantinople in 945. In 1020 Emperor Basilius II invaded Bulgaria, suppressed the patriarchate, and Achrida again became an archbishopric. Although as such she was independent of Constantinople, most of her prelates were Greeks: the archbishopric drifted away. About the beginning of the thirteenth century Achrida definitely joined the schism, and later adopted the Greek language in the liturgy.

In the meantime, about 1186, a patriotic movement succeeded in establishing a Bulgaria independent of the Byzantine Empire. Since the Bulgarian patriots could not request the establishment of a patriarchate from Constantinople, they turned to Pope Innocent III, who granted Basil, the Archbishop of Ternovo, the title of primate in 1204.

The union with Rome lasted till 1235, when political intrigues again entered the picture. The Bulgarians allied themselves with the Greeks against the Latin crusaders, and in 1235 the Patriarch of Constantinople, German II, recognized Ternovo as an independent patriarchate. This lasted till the Ottoman conquest in 1393, when the patriarchate was abolished and Ternovo was annexed to the archbishopric in Achrida.

From then until 1870 the Patriarch of Constantinople ruled supreme. The Slavonic language and customs were abolished, and the Greeks, who had dreamt of a Hellas covering the entire Balkan area, directed their opposition against all other nationalities—especially the Bulgars, the strongest and bitterest opponents of the Greek national idea.

Again politics decided the issue. The Bulgars wanted to be a "nation," but, to be a nation under the Turkish rule, there had to be a national church. Hence, the Bulgars approached the Armenian Catholic patriarch with the request that the Holy See receive them into the Church, guaranteeing them the use of the Slavonic language and their own canon law and customs. The negotiations were successful. Many abjured the schism and in 1861 Pope Pius IX himself consecrated their first Catholic bishop.

But Russia could not tolerate the Catholic Church in the Balkans, and, using all possible pressure, persuaded the Sultan to establish an Orthodox National Church for the Bulgars. The only thing the Bulgars wanted was to be a nation, and as soon as they found they could be one without the Pope, they gave up the idea of being Catholics. The Sultan established the Independent Orthodox Church in 1870. This Independent Church was excommunicated by the Patriarch of Constantinople in 1872. Thus, the Bulgarian Dissidents were formally in schism with Constantinople itself, and one of the principal reasons for it can be ascribed to corrupt politics. Recently, the Bulgarian Exarch Stefan has been reconciled with the Patriarch of Constantinople, thus ending the schism between the Bulgarian Dissident Church and Constantinople.

At present there are eleven Dissident metropolitans and several suffragan bishops who rule over 4,000,000 faithful. The Catholics of the Byzantine Rite have an Apostolic Administrator and an Apostolic Visitor who, with forty-one priests, minister to the faithful.

Intolerable political conditions prior to and following the Macedonian revolt in 1903 moved numerous Bulgarians, especially Macedonian Bulgarians, to seek refuge in the United States and Canada. Some reports state that at the present time about 65,000 Bulgarians are to be found here. Of these thirty to forty thousand are located in the urban areas of Illinois, Indiana, Michigan, New York, Ohio, and Pennsylvania. The majority apparently adhere to the Bulgarian Orthodox Church, while a small percentage of them have joined various Protestant denominations. The Orthodox element is grouped around a dozen or more churches theoretically subject to the jurisdiction of His Grace, Bishop Velichky, residing in New York City. This Bulgarian bishopric of New York was established by the Holy Synod of Bulgaria in January 1938, but only two or three of the churches submitted themselves to the rule of Bishop Velichky.

It is interesting to note that the report of the Holy Synod in Sofia, published by the United States Bureau of the Census with the approval of the Bulgarian Legation, makes no mention of the Catholic phases in the history of the Bulgarian Church. The same omission appears in another report on the Bulgarians—in Joseph S. Roucek's book, *One America.*

The history of the Yugoslavs, particularly the Serbians, is much the same as that of the Bulgars. Briefly, the Serbians were converted by Byzantine missionaries between 867 and 886, while the Croatians received the Gospel from the West. Between 1159 and 1204 the Serbians maintained relations with Rome and Constantinople; as a matter of fact, one of their most venerated archbishops, Archbishop Sava, consecrated by the Patriarch in Constantinople, in the year 1220 anointed his own brother, Stephen II Nemanja King of the Serbians in the name of Pope Honorius III. Later on, Greek and Turkish political machinations succeeded in destroying the Serbian Church. The Catholic Church of the Byzantine Rite was re-established in 1611, and it is from this group that the only Catholic Byzantine-Slavonic diocese in Yugoslavia was formed. Today the Serbs have one bishop[1] who governs 42,000 people with fifty-eight priests. There are five and a half million Dissidents under the supervision of one patriarch, three metropolitans and twenty-one bishops.

The mass immigration of the Serbian Dissidents into this country and Canada dates back to 1890. According to reports received from twenty-seven of the thirty-six churches now in existence in the United States, there are 20,000 Dissident Serbians settled in the urban areas of California, Illinois, Indiana, Minnesota, Missouri, Nebraska, New York, Ohio, Pennsylvania, and Wisconsin. At first, they were under the jurisdiction of the American Russian Orthodox hierarchy. In 1921 the Serbian patriarchate founded a special diocese for the United States and Canada, which received its first bishop in 1926. The official see of this Serbian diocese is located at the Serbian Monastery of St. Sava in Libertyville, Illinois, but at the present time the bishop resides in Chicago.

The most interesting history is that of the Russian

[1] It was authoritatively reported that the bishop died as a result of poison administered while he was imprisoned by Tito.

Church and the Churches that sprang from it; they play the leading part in the modern history of the Byzantine Church. After a rapid sketch of this Church, I shall examine the legends popularized among the Russians about the origin of Christianity in Russia. For the moment I should like briefly to note that the more level-headed and scholarly historians of Russia, headed by the Dissident Dr. Golubinsky, have discarded these legends and recognize that, while the general conversion of Russia in 988-89 during the reign of St. Vladimir was effected through Byzantine missionaries, the small communities of Catholics up to that time came into existence through the activities of Western missionaries.

It is true that Russia was converted by Constantinople. But there is little doubt that she looked upon Rome as the spiritual center of all Christians, and it was not till the latter part of the thirteenth century that Rome and Kiev, or rather what was left of that center of Russian ecclesiastical life, drifted apart. This was partially due to disorders following the Mongolian invasion, aided by the relentless propaganda of Greek bishops and priests who were infected by the germs of the Cerularian Schism. Although Russia maintained relations with Constantinople even after the Eastern Schism, for a short time she also maintained them with Rome. Thus, for instance, the legates who excommunicated Cerularius escaped through Kiev, and marriages between Russians and Catholics of the Latin Rite were numerous up to the early years of the twelfth century.

In 1239, Kiev, the center of ecclesiastical life and the see of the metropolitan, was razed by the Mongolians. As a result, the metropolitan see was transferred to Vladimir on the Kliazma. In 1325 it was again transferred to Moscow, still bearing the title of the Metropolitan of Kiev. The years following the Union brought about at the Council of Florence marks the definite separation of Moscow and Kiev as metropolitan sees. This period also witnessed the division in history between the Russians, later called Moscovites, staunch adherents of the Cerularian Schism, and the other Russians traditionally referred to as Ruthenians by the Holy See, the torchbearers of true Catholicism among the many Slavic nations of Russia. In 1509 the Tsar Feodor Ivanovitch forced the Patriarch of Constantinople, Jeremias II, to proclaim the Metropolitan of Moscow a patriarch no longer subject to Constantinople.

When Peter the Great came into power, he subjugated the Church for his own political purposes, shifted the center of his empire from Moscow to St. Petersburg, his new capital, abolished the patriarchate, and in its stead in the year 1721 commissioned the Holy Governing Synod to rule the

Russian Church. Degeneration in the Russian Church became the rule and continued for nearly two centuries, although determined attempts at reform were made at the turn of this century. These, however, were interrupted by the war.

After the Revolution of 1917, the patriarchate was again re-established in 1918 and ruled by a saintly man, Tikon. But intrigue and politics continued their destructive work. Tikon was imprisoned in 1922, the patriarchate abolished and a so-called Higher Church Administration established. This was followed by new schisms and disruptions, which resulted in further weakening of the Russian Church. The true status of the Church in Soviet Russia—that of a mere cog of the government—is today known to all.

America's first contact with the Russian Dissident Church dates back to the days when Russian explorers chanced upon the shores of Alaska and the Aleutian Islands. At the request of Shelikov, a Russian merchant who organized the first trading colony on the Island of Kodiak, the Holy Governing Synod of Russia sent a number of missionaries to Kodiak, and these in turn built the first Russian Dissident church in 1792. In the succeeding years, a number of additional missionaries were sent to Alaska, to care for the Russians and to do missionary work among the natives.

Of these, John Veniaminov, later known as Bishop Innocent, was the most prominent. He devised an alphabet, then translated the catechism, ritual, and several books of the Bible into the Aleutian language. In 1840 he was appointed Bishop of Alaska; he established his cathedral in Sitka, from whence he governed his flock, served about thirty churches and chapels.

Following the sale of Alaska to the United States, the episcopal see was moved from Sitka to San Francisco (1872), with jurisdiction over the entire West Coast. In 1891, Bishop Vladimir was succeeded by Bishop Nicholas, during whose stay the diocese was enlarged to include the whole of Canada and the eastern part of the United States. In 1905, the episcopal see was transferred from San Francisco to New York City and was elevated to the rank of an archdiocese with two suffragan bishops, one for the diocese of Alaska, and the other for the Syrian Mission with headquarters in Brooklyn, New York, headed by an Arabic-speaking bishop of the Russian jurisdiction. Later, additional suffragan bishoprics were established in Pittsburgh and Canada.

Today the Russian Dissident Church has eleven bishoprics in the United States, Canada, and Alaska, divided into twenty-five districts under district deans. The overall membership in the Russian Orthodox Church in America, as reported by the Census Bureau, is 89,510, divided among 229 churches. Considering the fact that the majority of these people are in reality former Catholics who have fallen into schism, one wonders what became of the 250,000 Russians reportedly living in this country.

The confusion resulting from the attempts on the part of the Soviet Government to control the Church in Russia was also reflected in this country. When Tikon, the Patriarch of Moscow, refused to subscribe to the policies of the Soviet government, the newly re-established patriarchate was abolished, Tikon was imprisoned, and many of his followers were either imprisoned, exiled, or executed as enemies of the state. But it was not long before the government realized that it could not destroy the Church in Russia by force. With the aid of the radical element of the clergy, the Soviet Government established a new Church in 1923, known as the Living Church. A representative of this group came to the United States, managed to obtain possession of St. Nicholas' Russian Cathedral in New York City, and created a schism within the Russian Dissident Church in this country. The Protestant Episcopal Church in New York City, however, turned over one of their chapels for the use of the evicted Metropolitan Platon, who had remained loyal to the Old Orthodox Church.

Aside from the Dissident element, a fairly large number

of Russians can be found scattered among many Protestant denominations. In addition to these, there are others who form various sectarian groups such as the Old Believers, Molokans, Dukhobors, and others.

To return to Kiev, its downfall was in preparation long before the Mongolian invasion, and was due to the political strife that began with the five sons of the Grand Prince Vladimir II (1113-25). The continuous dissensions made the Ruthenians an easy prey for the invading Lithuanians in 1340, when Kiev fell to Gedimin; and this was followed by the conquest of Podolia. Later on these provinces were annexed to Poland together with the province of Galicia. The Union of Florence of 1439 was accepted by Kiev and the many suffragan sees, but only lasted till 1517. Though the idea of reunion continued to bear occasional fruits, the hierarchy was in communion with Constantinople. As a result, the Ruthenian nobility embraced the Latin Rite, while the bulk of the Ruthenian Church was struggling in the death grip of schism.

In 1596 a new reunion with the Holy See, solemnly proclaimed at Brest-Litovsk, forecast a new period in the Ruthenian Church. It was a period of martyrdom, and also of steady progress. In 1623 St. Josaphat died a martyr's death. The year 1634 marks the date Kiev definitely returned to schism. Shortly afterwards came the hectic days of the Cossack Insurrection under Bogdan Khmelnitsky, which resulted in the partition of the Ukraine between Russia and Poland. With the first partition of Poland in 1772, White Russia passed under the Moscovite regime and more churches were forced into schism. The Church's sufferings increased with the years, for, with the absorption of more and more territory by the Russian Empire, many Catholics were lost. Ultimately, of the many churches flourishing in the former Principality of Kiev, only the churches in Galicia and a province of Austria and postwar Poland remained faithful to the Holy See. With more than five million faithful, these, with the Rusins of Carpatho-Russia form the bulk of the Catholic Byzantine-Slavonic Church.

We have another small group of Catholics of the Byzantine-Slavonic Rite south of the Carpathian Mountains. They, too, are descendants of the original Slavs of Kiev, since a great number of their ancestors left their homeland and migrated into Hungary, where they mingled with the so-called Eastern Slavs. This migration continued into the seventeenth century. These Slavs were in communion with Constantinople until their reunion with Rome, which got under way in 1646 under the guidance of their Bishop Peter Parthenius and Archbishop George Lippay, Primate of Hungary. This reunion spread from province to province until 1725. It culminated in the establishment of the diocese of Munkacs in 1771, by Pope Clement XIV. As in other instances, this period of reunion is also marked by martyrdom, for the Ruthenians suffered persecution at the hands of the Dissidents, Calvinists, and even the suspicious Catholics (not to mention the damage caused by political strife). The diocese of Munkacs became the mother of the Catholics of the Byzantine Rite in Hungary, and, as time passed by and the administration of the faithful became more and more difficult, the diocese was divided into several dioceses, all subject to the Latin Archbishop of Esztergom.

Following World War I, this little province joined the Czechoslovak Republic, and again was torn by religious strife brought on by political machinations and intense Dissident propaganda.

Two years ago, press despatches indicated that these millions of Catholics of the Byzantine-Slavonic Rite chose to incorporate themselves into the Union of Soviet Socialistic Republics, as an integral part of the Ukrainian Republic. Many thoughtful observers have believed that this would spell the end of the Catholic Church among these people.[2] Should Divine Providence allow this to happen,

[2] Thus far, every effort of the Soviet Government to force these people into schism has failed miserably. Defying torture, imprisonment, exile, or death, a number of communities which went into schism during the Czechoslovak regime publicly renounced schism and asked to be reinstated into the Catholic Church. See "The Ruthenian Tragedy," *Homiletic and Pastoral Review,* 46 (1946), 574-84.

the Catholic Byzantine-Slavonic Church in this country will be laden with the momentous duty of carrying on those sacred traditions until such time as our missionaries have the chance to bring about a rebirth of the Byzantine-Slavonic Church in those parts.

As we consider this matter, we cannot but admire and thank God's providence which some sixty years ago guided the Slavic Catholic immigrants to this country, dedicated to freedom, and inspired them to establish churches of their own. What courage this undertaking needed and what hardships had to be endured are known only to God. But in the end they were successful, and a fairly well-organized Church was established. It is now up to the Catholic community of America to help develop and preserve this Church for its great mission.

VI

RUSSIA AND THE FUTURE

SOME seventy years ago, Feodor Dostoyevski, the great Russian novelist, bitterly complained about the disdain which the Western civilized nations of Europe and the so-called "westernizing Russians" held for his native land. According to them, complained Dostoyevski, Russia was a mere barbaric land, awkwardly trying to find a place among other civilized nations.

While there might have been some truth in this, the situation since the times of Dostoyevski has certainly changed: Russia today monopolizes the headlines, in newspapers, magazines, and reviews. Russia is no longer the "window" through which the civilized world may gain a glimpse of the mysterious East, and the city once called St. Petersburg is no longer the "perch" from which the backward Russians might marvel at the progressive West. A few decades ago, thousands of Russians were straining every fiber to shed everything that labeled them as Russians. Today, thousands of non-Russians are straining every fiber to be like the Russians, and are scrambling for a seat on the Russian band wagon.

Russia, the great unknown quantity, has finally stirred; the colossus is on the march, and, with apprehension or admiration gripping their hearts, friend and foe have their eyes fixed on her. What will Russia do next? What influence will she exert on our lives?

These and similar thoughts are occupying the minds of many men and women throughout the world. And rightly so, for it would seem that the prophetic visions of such intellectual giants as the passionately Dissident Dostoyevski and the Catholic Soloviev stand a chance of being fulfilled, and that Russia may yet dominate completely the political, social, and even religious aspects of present-day history.

Amateurs as well as serious thinkers are agreed that the twentieth century will be remembered as a period dominated by Russia, while an ever growing number of scholars profess that the Russian Revolution is perhaps the most significant event in the history of mankind since the fall of the Roman Empire. It would be impossible to give a complete account of the influence Russian Communism has come to exert on the internal life of all nations. One thing is certain: this influence is evil. An excellent discussion on this point is given by William Thomas Walsh in the last chapter of his *Characters of the Inquisition.*

To give a few examples of this harmful influence, did not the great Marxian experiment in Russia loose the floods of the evil powers that brought on our present tragedy? Was it not the professed desire to stem the Bolshevik tide that brought forth Mussolini and his Fascism? Did not Hitler and his National Socialism gain power in Germany on the pretense of saving it from Bolshevism? Was it not the unrest fostered by the Kremlin revolutionaries that made masses of people lose faith in their respective governments' ability to solve their social problems? Was it not the alliance of Hitler and Stalin that made the recent cataclysm possible?

And on the other side of the ledger—to consider the ways in which Russia has influenced world affairs for good —was it not an invaded Russia that dealt the first mortal blow to the enemy, and prepared the way for victory?

Should these drops from the ocean of contemporary fact fail to convince us of the influence Russia has come to bear on our lives, we need but read the statements our Blessed Mother made to the world on July 13, 1917, in Fatima, Portugal, through her three little servants: "If people attend to my petition, Russia will be converted and there will be peace. Otherwise, an impious propaganda will spread its errors through the world, raising up wars and persecution against the Church. Many will be martyred; the Holy Father will have much to suffer; several nations will be destroyed."[1]

Dostoyevski and his followers visualized the union of all Slav nations under the powerful protection of a mighty Russia, but their motives were far different from those of Moscow today. He was well acquainted with the noble past of his country and passionately believed in what many of his nationals called the "divine" mission of the Dissident Russian Church. With others of his nation, he believed that Catholicism, like Acherontic Protestantism, failed in her religious mission, and was firmly convinced that only Orthodoxy (meaning the separated Church of the East) could help the floundering human race. It happened that pure and unadulterated Orthodoxy was no longer to be found in any other land except Russia. Russia, Dostoyevski concluded, must dominate the world, because only she can give and preserve true Orthodoxy. These very ideas, which form the basic principle of Russian ecclesiastical tradition, were at the bottom of the somewhat paradoxical statement of Sergei, the late Patriarch of Moscow, who claimed that

[1] V. Montes de Oca, *More About Fatima* (Dublin, 1945), 59.

henceforth Moscow would become the center of all religion.

Soloviev, justly considered the Russian Newman, was also a proponent of the Pan-Slav movement. But, following his conversion to the Catholic Church, his Pan-Slavism—his belief in the religious mission of Russia—became Catholic. Discussing the possibility of reunion between the Eastern and Western Churches in a memorandum submitted to Pope Leo XIII, Soloviev expressed his views in regard to Russia's future thus:

The reunion of Churches will prove equally profitable for both parties. Rome will have gained a pious and religiously enthusiastic people, she will have gained a powerful and faithful defender. Russia, which in accordance with the will of God holds the destinies of the East, will not only have freed herself of the sin of involuntary schism, but will eo ipso *become free to accomplish her great universal vocation, i.e., she will reunite all Slav nations and will establish a new civilization truly Christian, reuniting the characteristics of the one truth and the multiform freedom in the supreme principle of charity, which embraces all in unity and distributes to all the plenitude of the unique good.*[2]

[2] E. L. Radlov, *Pis'ma Vladimira S. Soloviev* (St. Petersburg, 1908), I, 183-90.

There can be no doubt that of the two conceptions, the Catholic and the Dissident, Soloviev had the right one, and Catholics, who believe in the divine institution and the divine mission of the Church, will not find it difficult to agree with him. Unfortunately for both Churches, the present horizon of human history is darkened by the cloud of a godless Bolshevism pledged to destroy religion in all forms. This godlessness appears to have taken a strong hold on the Russian community. As we view the present political developments in Europe, we witness the realization of the Pan-Slav dream, not along the lines of Dostoyevski's pattern or that of Soloviev, but along the lines of a Marxian "democracy" as interpreted by Stalin.

What can we hope to obtain from a power which, by its very essence, is pledged to destroy all religion, and especially its archfoe, the Catholic Church? Are there any grounds left for hoping that Russia will become a Catholic country, or at least opened to Catholic missionary efforts? Or that the Russian Dissident Church will return to Catholic unity?

Although the prospects are most discouraging at present, we cannot dismiss the thoughts Erik von Kühnelt-Leddihn has expressed in his novel, *The Gates of Hell.* In it, the admirable Father Scapinelli declares that the Bolsheviks have a twofold mission for the Catholic Church: "On the one hand you [i.e., the Bolsheviks] purge us of diseased elements, and on the other hand you are forerunners for us of the way. Thus did the Arians, for example, first infect the Ostrogoths with their Christian heretical faith, and then we simply Catholicized them. You have done genuine preliminary work for us. Believe me, there are ever so many Malays in Java who received their first Christian notions from your work. Where once the Agitation Bureaux of the Communist International have sown, the Propaganda of Faith will soon reap. That is precisely the tragedy of all heretics; they are forever doing productive work for the Mother Church from which alone they derive all their ideas after all. As an example of this, we are at present reaping the fruits of the Nestorians' mission in India. In five or six years they will all be petitioning the Holy Father for the Mass. . . ."

Many may disagree with these ideas, but, before they dismiss Russia as a bad bargain, they would do well to ponder the words of the Blessed Mother quoted above, as well as the last paragraph of that memorable prediction: "My Immaculate Heart will finally triumph."

Apparently, the realization of a true peace hinges on the conversion of Russia. There can be little doubt that the horrors of the Russian religious persecutions were permitted by God to cleanse the Russian Church of the cockle and prepare her for the great day of Reunion. Stalin will perhaps prepare the material stage for this great event by uniting the East—which, in the words of Soloviev, holds great possibilities for our civilization. But the spiritual change in Russia and in the separated Near East will have to come through the co-operation and best efforts of all Catholic nations.

The seeds of martyrdom have been sown in quantities that perhaps surpass those sown during the early Christian persecutions. For years now, these seeds have been watered by the fervent prayers of millions. Presently the laborers—and the one hundred million Catholics now under Soviet domination might well become their spearhead—must go forth and reap the harvest. But the success of this mission will be in sight only if we bring about a better understanding between the Eastern Christians and ourselves through a full comprehension of those vital forces which shaped their destinies.

For our part, we will not be able to gain an understanding of our Eastern brothers unless we study their—our own—past. The need for such a study was realized by Catholics when they were struggling against the Reformation, and this resulted in the conversion of such men as Newman and Chesterton. But the East, for some reason, is either forgotten or challenged by means unsuited to the purpose. Little wonder that, while the Church made considerable headway in the West, it made none in the East.

Once again let it be said that the remedy for this lies in making a penetrating study of the peoples of Russia and of the Near East; we will thus gain the means to span the chasm at present separating East and West, and will make possible a united effort against the powers of darkness and godlessness in Russia and the rest of the world.

Our Lady of Fatima declared that the peace of the world depends on the conversion of Russia. Pope Pius XI deemed this idea important enough to write a special encyclical, urging Catholic seminaries, universities, and other institutions of higher learning to establish special courses for the study of the Near East. Would not the Catholic cause and, in general, the cause of peace profit if our Catholic youth, the future leaders of Catholic thought and Catholic action, were given the opportunity to learn about Russia and the Near East under competent guidance in our Catholic schools?

High-ranking prelates here and abroad consider that, once peace is re-established, America will be called upon to furnish the Catholic religious leaders for Europe. But we will not be able to give competent and efficient leadership unless we have prepared ourselves for that work by an earnest study of Europe's past, and this study would be incomplete if it were to by-pass Russia and the lesser nations in the Near East—the Scylla and the Charybdis of European peace.

The rubble heap that was once Europe is still smoldering, the air is thick with the stench of decaying corpses and the acrid smell of gunpowder, the endless rows of military graves are not yet covered with grass, and already the foundations of the next war are being laid. In May 1946, a banquet was held in New York City in honor of the members of the United States Reparations Committee. It was reported that a member of this committee made a statement that ran somewhat like this:

The United States and Russia have solved the religious question within the Eastern portion of Europe. After these parts, i.e., the Baltic States, Poland, all of Eastern Germany, Czechoslovakia, Hungary, Rumania, Bulgaria, and Austria, have been forever incorporated as an integral part of the U.S.S.R., the religious question will in the future be regulated as follows: in all these parts of Europe the Russian Orthodox Church will be dominant under the leadership of Stalin. All Roman Catholics in the said territories will be severed from Rome and will be forced into the Russian Orthodox Church. The new Pope of the East will be the Patriarch of Moscow.

It makes little difference whether this individual spoke

as a private citizen or as an official of our country. In either instance his words illustrate what evils may yet be brought about by those ignorant of facts and the important part these facts play in shaping men's destinies. There are those who, as David J. Dallin points out in his scholarly works on Soviet Russia, succumb to wishful thinking and persuade themselves that Bolshevism is gradually, if imperceptibly, transforming itself into Democracy. A study of *The Origin of Russian Communism* by the Orthodox writer, Nicholas Berdyaev, would make clear to them how mistaken that notion is. The problem of Russia, like that of most of eastern Europe, is primarily a religious one, whose only solution lies in regaining complete possession of Christian faith and Christian principles.

VII

ORIGINS OF CHRISTIANITY IN RUSSIA

THE true origin of Christianity in Russia is still under debate. There are two theories in this regard: The Catholic theory, which claims that Russia was Catholic from the very beginning of its Christian era, and only later became separated from the Holy See; the Dissident theory —promoted by Russian textbooks on Russian history— which maintains that Russia had always been Orthodox, in the sense that she never acknowledged the supremacy of Rome.

The Dissident theory is based on a legend to be found in the extant manuscripts of Russia's first chronicles. Prince Vladimir of Kiev, according to this legend, decided to renounce his pagan gods and interviewed emissaries of various nations to find a suitable religion for himself and his people. On learning that the Moslems were not permitted the use of wine, Vladimir dismissed them, saying: "Russia delights in drinking; we cannot do without it." Nor was he satisfied with the report of the Jewish emissaries, who were forced to admit that they lost their country through the wrath of God. The report of the Christian emissaries impressed him, but, before making a decision, he sent his own emissaries to Rome and Constantinople to study the Christian observance. The emissaries, on their return, reported that the ceremonies and observances of Rome did not appeal to them at all, but that their experiences in Constantinople were particularly inspiring. The emissaries told Vladimir that on entering the church of St. Sophia in Constantinople they could not tell "whether they were on earth or in heaven," since on earth "so great a spectacle and so much beauty could not be seen." Vladimir decided that the religion of Constantinople was the true religion and, on July 15, 988, he and his people were received into the Orthodox Church through baptism administered on the banks of the Dnieper River.

Despite officious Russian ecclesiastical censors, Russia's prerevolutionary scholars have admitted that the story of Russia's conversion as it now reads in the extant manuscripts of the early chronicles is not genuine, but represents a later interpolation by partisans who wished to confirm the Orthodox position against the claims of Rome.

Catholic scholars maintain that the origins of Christianity in Russia are steeped in Catholic tradition. This theory is substantiated by several irrefutable facts: (1) Vladimir and Russia received Christianity in 988, i.e., sixty-six years before Michael Cerularius, the Patriarch of Constantinople, denounced the Holy See and gave birth to what is now known as the Eastern Schism; (2) the numerous intermarriages between Russian and Western Catholic nobility indicate a community of faith between the Catholic West and the newly converted Russia; (3) there exists today a fairly large collection of correspondence between the Holy See and the princes of Russia, as well as other documents of that early period, which support the claim that Russia was originally a Catholic country.

Undoubtedly, the question of Russia's Christian origin is fraught with difficulties, for, despite the evidence which points to Russia's Catholic origin, there are on the other hand documents which seem to indicate the opposite.

But let us look deeper into the story of Russia's conversion. The political entity which occupied the basin between Lake Ilmen and the Dnieper River was known in the ninth century as Rus. The population of this country was composed of several Slavonic tribes ruled by Varangian Vikings. From the religious standpoint, the Russians of the pre-Christian era can be classified as nature worshippers. Under the able rule of the descendants of Rurik, Rus built up a prosperous trade in defense of which she was often compelled to wage war against her neighbors, and more than once did her warriors pound the gates of mighty Constantinople.

In view of these intense commercial relations and frequent military expeditions, Rus came into close contact with the Catholic West, the turbulent Southeast, and the Moslem East. Hence, it is not surprising to find, among others, Catholic churches, Catholic missionaries, and isolated Catholic groups almost at the very beginning of Rus. In the year 862 the Varangian leader Rurik laid the foundations of mighty Rus—the nucleus of the Russian Empire; five years later, Photius, who precipitated one of the schisms of the East, assures us that a bishop and several missionaries were sent to Rus and worked among the natives with some success. Ninety-five years later, in 957, Olga, Grand Duchess of Kiev and the grandmother of Vladimir, received baptism from the hands of Theophylactus, Patriarch of Constantinople.[1] Notwithstanding the many and fairly successful inroads made by Christianity, the bulk of the people of Rus continued to worship their pagan gods.

In 988, Vladimir, Prince of Kiev, led a military expedition against the Greek colony of Chersonesus in Taurica and was victor. Among other things, the peace terms stipulated that Vladimir could marry the Princess Anna, sister (or better, perhaps, cousin) of the Byzantine emperor, Basil II, provided Vladimir became a Christian. Vladimir accepted the offer and forthwith was baptized in Chersonesus. Upon his return to Kiev he ordered the destruction of all idols and the baptism of all his subjects. To provide for the spiritual ministrations, Constantinople agreed to send bishops and priests. Later, bishoprics were established in the principal cities—Kiev, Novgorod, Rostov, Yaroslav, and Tchernigov. The son and successor of Vladimir, Yaroslav I, persuaded the Patriarch of Constantinople to promote the Bishop of Kiev to the rank of Metropolitan of all Russia. This was effected in the year 1035.

These are the principal facts relating to the conversion of Russia as they now appear in the extant manuscripts of the early Russian chronicles, and, with the exception of the actual baptism of Vladimir, they are generally accepted by Catholic and Dissident historians.

As for Vladimir's baptism, there is a more probable and less romantic story which can be summarized as follows. Aside from influences exerted by neighboring Christian nations, politico-social interests, and the inherent no-

[1] According to several Greek accounts, Olga visited Constantinople in the company of a priest named Gregory, who was her confessor. If these accounts are true, Olga was a Christian before her visit to Constantinople.

bility of Christianity itself which must have impressed Vladimir, he was undeniably influenced by his Norwegian friend Olaf Tryggvasson. It is a well-established fact that Olaf had not only become a convert, but, as Christopher Dawson states, set himself to spread the faith in characteristically Viking fashion. It is generally admitted that Olaf, whom Vladimir had saved from certain death, exerted great influence on Vladimir; hence it is more than probable that it was at the urging of this Norwegian King that Vladimir consented to be baptized. How, when, and by whom this baptism was performed, no one can tell. Some recognized Dissident historians simply state that it is probable that Vladimir was baptized three years before his expedition against Crimea. At least one Catholic historian is of the opinion that Vladimir was baptized in 987 at Kiev at the hands of Latin Varangian missionaries. In addition to this, it should be remembered that Vladimir spent considerable time among the Catholic Bulgarians and there may have been attracted to Christianity.

The account of Vladimir's campaign against Crimea as it appears in the chronicles is incorrect, for it has been definitely established that he undertook the campaign at the invitation of Emperor Basil to help quell the rebellion of Varda Phocas, with the understanding that he was to receive certain valuables and Princess Anna as a wife.

Aside from these considerations it cannot be denied that Russia as a whole did receive Christianity through the good offices of Constantinople. But this does not necessarily mean that the original Church in Russia was a Church which did not recognize the Holy See as the center of Christianity. Catholic historians take the position that the original Church did recognize the Holy See, and they support their claims by the following facts.

Russia received Christianity in the year 988 at a time when Christendom was united. The misunderstanding which arose during the patriarchate of Photius was settled and, for all practical purposes, unity and good will reigned once more between Constantinople and Rome. In view of this circumstance, it was not surprising to see emissaries of Pope John XV presenting Vladimir with the skull of the martyred Pope St. Clement. The martyrdom of St. Clement probably took place at Chersonesus, the site of Vladimir's conversion, and his skull was found by St. Cyril, the Apostle of the Slavs, who donated this precious relic to the Holy See. Only because there was no dissension in Christendom could one explain the fact that papal emissaries were received "with great love and honor" at the court of Vladimir in Kiev in the year 991 and again in 1000, or of the newly converted prince sending Russian emmissaries to the papal court at Rome in the years 994 and 1001, returning the papal courtesy.

If Rus had been inimical to the Holy See, how can we explain the attested fact that Vladimir's successor, Yaroslav I, approached Pope Benedict VIII with the request that an archbishop be appointed to Kiev, and that this petition was followed by the papal appointment of a Bulgarian named Alexis? It is just as much of an attested fact that Prince Yaroslav I severed his relationships with Constantinople in the year 1051, and that the papal legates returning from Constantinople after the excommunication of Michael Cerularius, the Patriarch of Constantinople, in 1054, were received with "great honors" by the prince and populace of Kiev.

Russian Dissident scholars do not deny that side by side with the Greek clergy many Bulgarian clerics were ministering to the Russian faithful. These Bulgarian priests were Catholics, and it was through them that many Western Catholic elements were introduced into the juridico-social and religious life of early Christian Russia. Through them the Russians received the Bulgarian Nomocanon—a civil and ecclesiastical code of laws—in which it is clearly stated that the Pope is the head of the Church and in which the Chalcedonian claims of 451, which stated that the Patriarch of Constantinople is equal in dignity and power with the Pope of Rome, are energetically rejected as heretical.

In the period under discussion, intermarriages between Catholic and non-Catholic princes were practically unheard of. Yet marriages between Western Catholic and Russian princes took place frequently.

We possess a number of writings compiled in Russia during the eleventh, twelfth, and thirteenth centuries by schismatical or schismatically inclined ecclesiastics, in which they admonish the Russian faithful not to attend religious services and, above all, not to receive Holy Communion in the local Latin churches. This clearly indicates that the Russians were in the habit of attending religious services and receiving Holy Communion in Latin churches.

But can we conceive of local Catholic priests, who were certainly informed of the religious affiliation of the Russian people, permitting non-Catholics to receive Holy Communion in Catholic churches?

During the internecine wars which followed upon the death of Yaroslav the Wise (*d.* 1054), we find an interesting episode which also speaks of the Catholic convictions of the early dukes of Rus.

In 1068, Isyaslav I was defeated by the Polovtsi, Kiev's perennial enemies, and was forced to seek refuge in the household of Boleslav the Bold, of Poland. Taking advantage of this circumstance, Isyaslav's younger brother Svyatoslav took possession of Kiev and proclaimed himself Grand Duke of Rus. With the aid of Bolesav, Isyaslav regained his throne in 1069, but in 1073 was again forced into exile by Svyatoslav. On this occasion Isyaslav appealed to the German Emperor Henry IV for aid, and sent a delegation headed by his son Yaropolk-Peter to Pope Gregory VII, with instructions to submit all of Rus to the patronage of St. Peter and to obtain the Pope's support in his dispute.

The Pope wrote both to King Boleslav the Bold, who this time allied himself with Svyatopolk against Isyaslav, and to Svyatopolk, instructing both to step aside and acknowledge Isyaslav as the rightful Grand Duke of Rus.

There is one other important fact that makes the Dissident theory of Russia's conversion hard to accept. It is well known that Russia adopted the Slavonic version of the Byzantine Rite, despite the fact that Greek bishops and Greek priests were in charge of the newly established Russian Church. Dr. Golubinsky, Russia's foremost church historian and a loyal son of the Orthodox Church, assures us that, while the Holy See approved the Slavonic translation of the liturgy made by Sts. Cyril and Methodius, Constantinople vehemently opposed it. Keeping in mind this statement and the fact that it was made by a Russian Orthodox scholar, one cannot but ask this question: If Russia did not recognize the Holy See as the supreme judge in all matters religious, how could she have adopted the Slavonic liturgy approved by Rome, but looked upon with great disfavor by Constantinople—the Mother Church? If Russia looked upon Constantinople as the true leader and sole custodian of Christianity and held Rome in contempt, could she possibly have adopted a liturgy disfavored by Constantinople and sanctioned by her religious rival?

In view of these and similar historical facts, Catholic scholars appear justified in maintaining that the primitive Russian Church was really and truly Catholic. It is clear historically that Russia's misfortunes began when, under pressure of several political factors and under the relentless drive of Greek propaganda, she drifted away from the Common Father and, as a consequence, lost her vitality. This tragic circumstance, however, is not without a consolation. The Russian Church, the largest non-Catholic Christian body as such in the world, never officially quarreled with Rome; the early ties of cordiality and filial submission were never formally denounced. This fact should make it much easier to reunite the Church of Russia with her true mother, the Church of Rome.

Klyuchevski, Russia's classic historian, reflecting upon Russia's Kievan period—the period in which we claim Russia was Catholic—has this to say:

Russian historians and the Russian population gener-

ally have never failed to treat the memory of bygone Kiev with a sympathy hard to understand when we consider the chaotic impression produced upon the mind by a study of its greatest period. Not only are there few traces of Kievan Rus and its condition of life to be found now surviving in our land, but one would naturally suppose that the traditions of Kiev itself, with its incessant turmoil, its never-ending princely feuds and its struggle with the pagans of the Steppes, would have left anything but a grateful impression upon the popular mind. Yet many a poetical and religious legend has been preserved concerning the ancient seat of St. Vladimir, including the proverb that, as to Rome, all roads lead to Kiev. The Russian nation still knows and remembers the city of princes and heroes, of the Cathedral of St. Sophia and the Cloister of Petcherski, and loves and reverences its memory above that of any of the subsequent capitals of the land. Vladimir on the Kliazma has long ago been forgotten of the people, to whom it was never really known. Moscow only oppressed the people, and so was feared and respected, but not loved. As for St. Petersburg, it is neither feared nor respected nor loved. On the other hand, Kiev, with all its faults and failings, has never lost its hold upon the popular affections, and historians, whatever their school, have always agreed in painting the bygone life of the city in the brightest colors.[2]

[2] *History of Russia,* I, 124-25.

If Klyuchevski correctly appraised the Russian mind regarding the Kievan period of its history, if the Russians still yearn for the return of Kievan days, then it is important for us to be thoroughly acquainted with that period. For, if the Russians can be brought to realize that the Church of Kiev was Catholic, perhaps they will yearn for a return to the Mother Church. Again, Klyuchevski assures us that in those bygone days "the term Greek had come to be synonymous, in Rus, with the term rogue," and thus gave rise to a saying "He was full of guile because he was a Greek."[3]

He goes on to claim that Christian Russia did not think much of the Greek Church and suspected its orthodoxy. Given these facts, the Russians ought not find it overwhelmingly difficult to realize that, victimized by the "guile" of their early misguided Greek pastors, they were led away from the refreshing oasis of the Catholic fold to the desert of schism, but that the Catholic fold is where they truly belong.

[3] *Ibid.*, 178.

VIII

RUSSIA AND THE SCHISM

VLADIMIR Soloviev, the great Russian convert and philosopher, bitterly deplored the fact that his native country received Christianity through the ministrations of Constantinople. Like others before him, Soloviev believed that Russia's adherence to the Church of Byzantium excluded her from the vital evolutionary processes of European civilization, and that as a result Russia had necessarily to run a course of almost complete isolation.

It is not my purpose to analyze and pass judgment on this opinion. I note it simply to show that even though hope for an early reunion of the Russian Church with the Holy See appears to be premature, there have existed and there exist today among the Russians certain groups who believe that Russia's salvation depends upon her ability to free herself of the paralyzing spell of Byzantium.

We must remember that Russia's
conversion was not due, as in other countries in Northern

Europe, to the zeal of individual apostles, great missionaries who, crucifix in hand, penetrated into dense forests to preach the Gospel to wild Teutonic warriors. Russia received as her State religion the complete Christian faith, with an organized and impressive hierarchy in whose wake came artists who proceeded to build magnificent churches glittering with rich mosaics. In Russia Christianity became primarily a cult appealing to the feeling for beauty, and it is thus that it entered deeply into the national soul, awakening its artistic temperament and subjugating it for good.

Yet, something was lacking in this imposing worship—it had no moral depth, no power to move the soul to new duties beyond a call to sensible beauty—this is why Russian Christianity remained for so long superficial, a thin veneer of Christian ideas covering the simple and robust paganism of the masses with its superstitions, worship of the forces of nature curiously blended with devotion to the saints.[1]

This fact alone would suffice to explain how Russia, so recently converted to the Catholic Church, could follow Constantinople into schism. Having received little or no dogmatic training, the masses of the faithful firmly believed that the essence of Christianity consisted in the elaborate Byzantine ritual, and thus were easily swayed

[1] J. N. Danzas, *The Russian Church* (New York, 1936), 2-3.

by the adherents of schism. By making an issue of the ritual differences which existed between Rome and Constantinople, it was easy to convince the newly converted Russians that Rome, with its plain and practical ritual, was not truly Christian and should, therefore, be rejected as heretical. Thus it happened that Russia, though Catholic in origin, drifted away from, and became imbued with an undying hatred for, Rome. And though the Russians mistrusted and disliked the Greeks and their own Greek clergy, they had no choice but to look upon Constantinople as the true center of Christianity. For this reason we find no trace of any bitter dispute between the Holy See and Russia, at least nothing that could compare with the dispute which accompanied the schism of Cerularius in the East and the Reformation in the West.

Political disorders accelerated this regrettable separation between Rome and the Russian Church. The internecine quarrels among the princes of Russia that resulted from the complicated system governing the succession to the throne of the grand prince of Kiev, the sacking of Kiev by Andrew Bogolyubski, prince of the minor province of Suzdal, the Mongolian invasion that followed this sacking in 1239—all combined to hasten the parting of the ways between the Holy See and Russia. When Kiev fell to the Mongolians, Maxim, Metropolitan of Kiev, moved his see to Vladimir on the Kliazma, a small provincial town located east of Moscow and the capital of Suzdal.

Vladimir on the Kliazma had nothing to offer as a reminder of the early Catholic tradition of the Russian Church. As a matter of fact, the geographic and ethnographic conditions of this new religious center, together with the ruins of the ancient political and religious center of Russia, helped to confirm the exclusively ritualistic character of Russia's religion. This religion mechanically assimilated itself with some of the customs of the neighboring heathen Finnish tribes without Christianizing them, as was done in the West.

The traditions of Catholic Kiev were further obscured when the metropolitan see, still bearing the title of Kiev, was in 1325 transferred once again—to Moscow—and became known as the Metropolitan of Moscow.

All during these happenings the Holy See was not standing by complacently; it was making every effort to check this separatist movement. The Popes wrote innumerable letters to the ruling princes, inviting them to remain steadfast in or to return to the Catholic fold; missionaries were sent into the interior of Russia to keep up the Catholic traditions. And, with the rise of the Society of Jesus, there is hardly a decade in the history of Russia where one fails to find a Jesuit missionary trying to arrange a reconciliation between Moscow and the Holy See.

Even Peter the Great, whose duplicity in religious matters is very difficult to explain, seems to have considered the possibility of accomplishing the long-desired reunion. On two occasions he sent representatives to the Holy See to discuss the matter with Pope Clement XI, and as proof of his good intentions he promised safe conduct to Catholic missionaries passing through Russia, consented to the erection of a Capuchin monastery and other schools in Moscow, and promised freedom of worship to Catholics in his realm. These negotiations were unfortunately interrupted by the Pope's death.

At the beginning of the nineteenth century, Pope Pius VII started negotiations with Tsar Paul I, and offered to journey to St. Petersburg to discuss the reunion personally. Once again, the death of a Pope intervened and all of these efforts came to nothing.

In 1439, at the Council of Florence, among other representatives of the separated Eastern Churches, we find Isidore, the Metropolitan of all Russia. In the name of the Russian Church he, too, had signed the agreements which consummated the reunion of Churches. But on his return to Moscow he was greeted with the fury of the prince, the nobles, the clergy, and the people of Moscow, who would not hear of reunion. Imprisoned, he later escaped to Rome, where he died as a cardinal of the Catholic Church. This episode has considerable significance in the history of the Russian Church, and will be discussed shortly.

The fall of Constantinople to the Turks in 1453, together with the military success of Moscow against the Tartars in 1480, gave a new impulse to the forces proposing to set up Moscow as a third Rome. The princes of Moscow assumed the title of Tsars, the Russian counterpart of the Roman emperors, and in 1589 Jeremias II, Patriarch of Constantinople, was compelled to invest Job, the Moscovite Metropolitan, as first Patriarch of Moscow. Two years later this action was confirmed by the concurrence of the other patriarchs of the East, giving Moscow the fifth place after the Patriarchate of Jerusalem. The patriarchate functioned for one hundred and ten years and had eleven patriarchs. It was during this period that a momentous event took place in the history of the Russian Church.

During the centuries that had elapsed since the conversion of Russia, the liturgy of the Russian Church became corrupted with all sorts of inaccuracies. Aside from other causes too numerous to mention here, this was due to the fact that a great number of the early Russian clergy in rural districts could barely read and write, and, consequently, celebrated the Liturgy and other sacred functions mostly from memory. The need for a liturgical reform was acknowledged by the more erudite members of the clergy. At last the Patriarch Nikon, a prominent figure in Russian ecclesiastical history, revised the Slavonic liturgical books on the basis of the Greek liturgical books of Constantinople.

Even though Nikon's reforms were confirmed by a synod held in 1654, a large number of the clergy and the faithful —among them men of great sanctity—repudiated Nikon's reforms, thus creating a schism within the Russian Orthodox Church. These are known in history as the Raskolniks, or Old Believers, and were estimated to number about 20,000,000 members, with numerous churches and a fully organized hierarchical system. For centuries they were subjected to a most cruel persecution on the part of the Tsarist government.

The reforms of Nikon, however, were not the real cause for the breakdown of the unity of the Russian Church. For many years the spirit of the Western Reformation had been gaining ground among the Russians. It was a matter of course that in the wake of the Raskolniks there should spring up various sects, such as the Dukhobortsy—wrestlers of the spirit, some of them can be found in Canada, Sabbatarians, Dirkovtsy, who prayed before a hole in the wall, and Molokany, who took nothing but milk in Lent, a number of whom can be found in Los Angeles.

When Patriarch Adrian died in 1700, Tsar Peter the Great, who now aimed at the secularization of Russia and the total destruction of the Church, forbade the election of a new patriarch, and after a delay of twenty-one years gave the Russian Church a new Constitution. On the basis of this new Constitution, which was enforced until the revolution of 1917, the Russian Church was placed under the complete control of the so-called Holy Governing Synod. The members of this synod were appointed and removed at the will of the Tsar, and were under the complete control of a lay procurator, a minister of the crown.

The immediate result of these reforms was that the Russian Orthodox Church became a tool, and her clergy enslaved officials, of the State. While it is true that from time to time there were men who rebelled against this tyranny of the State, the Orthodox Church in Russia became so weak that nothing could halt its deterioration, and a considerable number of her faithful lost contact with true Christianity.

Political developments in 1905 forced the Government to grant religious freedom. This action initiated a religious revival which promised to bring about the desired reunion between the Holy See and the Church of Russia. Unfortunately, the revolution of 1917 put an end to this hope. The patriarchate was temporarily restored. But, as the Bolsheviks could tolerate no religion, they launched a great and bloody persecution in which hundreds of thousands of Russian Christians died for their belief in Christ. The blood of these real martyrs, acknowledged as such by Pope Pius XI, is the guarantee that the day of reunion cannot fail to come.

It has been previously pointed out that the events surrounding the Florentine Council had a great significance in the ecclesiastical history of Russia. On the one hand, the Union of Florence was the remote cause of the Union of Brest-Litovsk (1596), which gave birth to the Ruthenian Catholic Church. On the other hand, the fact that the Greeks at one time acknowledged the Pope as the Vicar of Christ confirmed the Russians in their belief that they have been called to take over the leadership in the Church of Christ. Always despised and mistrusted by the Russians, the Greeks taught the Russians from the very beginning of their conversion to hate Rome and to consider the Holy Father the incarnation of Antichrist.

When the Russians learned that the Greek Church had submitted to the supreme jurisdiction of the Holy See at the Council of Florence, they considered this an act of apostasy. To them, the fall of Constantinople to the Turks was a divine chastisement. It was almost inevitable that the Russians, who became heirs to an empire similar to the Byzantine Empire, should look upon themselves as the heirs of the true leadership in the Church of Christ. The idea of Moscow as a third Rome was widely held, not only by the clergy, but also by the literary and political leaders of Russia.

Thus, Russian political and ecclesiastical leaders considered it Russia's sacred mission to recapture Constantinople from the Turks, unite all Slavs under the arm of Russia's might, convert them to the Orthodox Church and, with this unified power, start a mighty crusade to convert the whole world to the Orthodox Church.

In view of the present political situation, it might be that God, in His infinite wisdom, is preparing the stage for that mighty crusade—with the sole difference that it will be aimed at the sacred cause of reunion between East and West. The millions of Catholics who have been absorbed by the Soviet State might turn out to be the spearhead of this crusade. Hence, the importance that we pray more than ever that God enlighten the mind of those in whose power it is, with God's grace, to heal the great rift created a thousand years ago.

IX

DOCTRINE OF THE RUSSIAN CHURCH

MANY Catholics, lay and ecclesiastic, are under the impression that the teachings of the Russian Dissident Church contain a number of errors directly opposed to the defined dogma of the Catholic Church. Hence, they place the Russian Orthodox Church in the same class as the Protestant Churches. This mistaken conception of the doctrinal position of the Russian Church is largely due to the numerous authors who wrote mistakenly on this subject. Among other things we are told that the Russian Dissident Church teaches five distinct heresies: (1) that the Holy Ghost proceeds *not* from the Father and the Son, but merely from the Father; (2) that the transubstantiation of bread and wine into the Body and Blood of our Lord *does not* take place at the moment the sacred words of the Institution are uttered, but only after the so-called Epiclesis has been recited; (3) that the Holy Father *is not* the visible head of the Church and the Vicar of Christ on earth; (4) that there *is no* Purgatory; (5) that the Blessed Mother *was not* preserved free from the stain of original sin at the moment of her conception.

While it is true that these statements can be found in most textbooks used in Russian seminaries, the fact remains that the doctrines of the Catholic and Russian Dissident Churches are identical, although in some instances those held by the Orthodox Church are not defined as clearly and adequately as they are in the Catholic Church today.

This position of the Russian Church has been brilliantly propounded by the great Russian convert, Vladimir Soloviev, in his "Memorandum" submitted to Pope Leo XIII. Since I consider this document one of the best expositions on the subject, I will take the liberty to quote at length from it:

The Oriental Church never determined and never presented to the belief of the faithful as an obligatory dogma *any doctrine contrary to the Catholic truth. The dogmatic decisions of the first seven ecumenical councils represent the sum total of absolutely indubitable and unchangeable doctrinal truths, recognized as such at all times and universally by the Oriental Church in its entirety. Anything that goes beyond these limits is subject to controversy [among the Orthodox] and can be considered as a particular doctrine of a certain theological school, or of an individual theologian of greater or lesser repute, which never received the sanction of the authority of an infallible magistry.*

The acts of some particular councils (held after the separation of the Churches) and certain catechisms (such as that of Peter Moghila of Kiev or that of Philaret of Moscow), notwithstanding the reputation they may enjoy, never received the supreme and definitive sanction of the Orthodox Church which could not transform their doctrines into articles of faith unless they made use of the infallibility of an ecumenical council which the Orthodox Church could not assemble because of her present isolation. Thus it is that our Church [the Orthodox Church] is not in possession of any symbolic book, taken in the sense in which this term is used by Catholics or Protestants. Some forty years ago, a German Protestant published, under the title, Libri Symbolici Ecclesiae Orientalis *[Symbolic books of the Eastern Church, this title later was changed to read* Monumenta Fidei Ecclesiae Orientalis*], a collection of documents of different periods and of different merit, and among others one document definitely heretical and generally recognized as such by us [the Oriental Confession by*

Patriarch Cyril Loukaris, well known for his Calvinistic sympathies].

This collection of M. Kimmel evidently does not possess any semblance of ecclesiastical authority and is known only to specialists. Shortly after its publication, our government published a code of ecclesiastical laws (in the Greek, Church Slavonic and modern Russian languages) under the title "Book of Rules" [Kniga Pravil], *which, together with the disciplinary canons of the Apostles, councils, and several Fathers, venerated by the Universal Church, contains also the truths of the Orthodox faith, i.e., those which were formulated in the two councils (of Nicea and Constantinople) and in the three definitions* (opoi) *of the fourth, sixth and seventh ecumenical councils. It is evident that this official code of our Church does not contain any error, or any anti-Catholic element.*

It is an established fact that the opinions of our Oriental theologians, which are more or less contrary to the Catholic truth, in general are not proclaimed as infallible or obligatory dogmas *by these theologians themselves, nor are they accepted as such by the faithful, nor do they have the same value as the decisions of the ecumenical councils; consequently, it is quite evident that one cannot justly place the responsibility for the anti-Catholic teachings of our theo-*

logians on the Oriental Church, as a body, since she never gave these doctrines her definitive sanction.

The distinction which is made between a doctrine of a certain theological school and the doctrine of a church, to which that school may belong, is applicable to a certain extent to Catholicism as well. To quote but one instance, it is known to all that for centuries the great theological school of the Thomists and the great Dominican Order attacked, or at least refused to recognize the sublime truth of the Immaculate Conception of the Most Holy Virgin, maintaining that she also was tainted with original sin. But who would have the audacity to blame the Catholic Church for this error of otherwise highly respected theologians, who, in this particular instance, gave expression to their personal opinions?

As for the masses of the faithful of the Oriental Church, one cannot accuse them of any definite error, seeing that their faith is the same as the Catholic Faith save for their ignorance of a few doctrinal definitions that are principally concerned with the true character and the attributes of the supreme power in the Church determined in the West after the separation was accomplished; this ignorance which can be more easily excused since this chapter of Catholic doctrine was not definitely fixed and not definitely explained by the Western Church herself until very recent times, i.e., till the last council held at the Vatican.

It is clear, therefore, that this distinction between the doctrine of the Church as such and the doctrine of a school or of individual theologians is most helpful in the cause of Reunion of Churches. As a matter of fact, the dogmas of our [*Orthodox*] Church *can be reduced to the decisions of the ecumenical councils, and, consequently,* are in fact Orthodox and Catholic, *and the doctrines of theologians which contradict Catholicism are not dogmas of faith determined by the Church. And thus we are united with Catholicism, because we ourselves recognize these truths as absolute and unchangeable, while the errors which separate us from Catholic unity are nothing but opinions reft of all superior authority, as the authors and abettors of these opinions will readily acknowledge.*

On the other hand one must not forget, and this is a very grave and advantageous circumstance for the cause of Reunion, that as regards the relationship towards the Catholic Church, within the Oriental Church there is no internal accord, no unity of thought. Since the separation of the Churches no ecumenical councils were held in the East and, according to the opinion of our better theologians, none an be held, the causes leading to separation were never judged by a competent authority, which would be recognized as such; thus it is that our schism exists only de facto, *but by no means* de jure. "Adhuc sub judice lis est."

In view of this state of affairs, one should not wonder at the extreme variety of diverse and contradictory opinions professed by the Russian and Greek theologians in regard to Catholicism. While there were some writers (fortunately few in number) averring that Catholicism not only strayed from the true Church, but in general betrayed Christianity as well, other personages more authoritative and more competent [as for instance the present Metropolitan of Kiev, the venerable Msgr. Platon] publicly declared that the Eastern and Western Churches were twin sisters separated only by a misunderstanding.

Between these two extreme views one will find, in our theological literature, all possible nuances of positive and negative views, views of sympathy and antipathy in regard to the Western Church.

Aside from these differences of opinion among the individual theologians, there is also a great contrast in the manner in which the Catholics are treated by the Russian Church and by the Greek [Hellenic] Church. While the Greeks, as if to mock their own attempts at reunion, still maintain the absurd and sacrilegious custom according to which they rebaptize all Western Christians who desire to affiliate themselves with their [Orthodox] Church (making no distinction between Catholics and Protestants), in Russia, on the contrary, not only is baptism of all Western Christians recognized as valid, but, insofar as the Catholic Church is concerned, we [Orthodox] also recognize the validity of the other Sacraments administered by Catholics, particularly the Sacrament of Holy Orders. Consequently, when Catholic bishops and priests are received into our Church, they are allowed to retain their ecclesiastical dignity. And what is more remarkable, when in 1839 the reunited Ruthenians were forced to join the dominating Church of Russia, the people *were not requested to abjure their Catholic beliefs.*

In view of these facts we feel safe in concluding that the Russian Church not only recognizes the efficacy of grace in the Catholic Church, but also recognizes the absence of any dogmatic error or heresy in the Catholic teaching. And if at the same time one finds in Russia a group of so-called Orthodox writers, recognized as such by certain group of the clergy, which revives the ancient injuries of heretics declaring that Catholicism is nothing else than anti-Christianism, etc., this represents but one other instance in a long series of contradictions which in the long run will be of great advantage to the cause of reunion. In fact, these contradictions, once they are recognized, will necessarily pro-

voke an interior stimulus *which will force us* [*Orthodox*] *to bring the question into full light in an endeavor to solve it. Once public attention, in all seriousness, will have been called to the abnormal state of our religious and ecclesiastical affairs, something definite will have to be done. And because it is quite certain that in this matter one will find more ignorance than bad will, in order that a solution* in principle *be reached it will suffice to clarify the problem in the pure light of truth and scholarship.*

As for the practical solution of the problem, there is one favorable circumstance to consider, namely, that the Oriental Church, and in particular the Russian Church, never did belong to the Western Patriarchate, and thus the uniform centralization of ecclesiastical power, as developed in the limits of the Latin Church, in its entirety cannot be imposed in our midst. The present constitution of the Catholic Church to a certain extent has been determined by the deplorable Eastern schism which for centuries limited Catholic activities to the Latin Patriarchate exclusively, in which the Universal Church had to gain in unity what it had lost in extension. Sed pereunte causa tolitur effectus. *Once ancient unity is re-established, the Catholic Church, remaining* forever Roman *because of her center of unity, will no longer be entirely Latin and Western as it is now because of uniformity in organization and administration* (*notwithstanding the tolerance of other rites which actually play but a secondary part*). Romana *is the name of the center which is equally and unchangeably the center of the whole circumference;* Latina *designates but one-half, one great section of the circle which should never definitely absorb the whole. It is the Church of Rome, not the Latin Church, that is the* "Mater et magistra omnium ecclesiarum"; *it is the Bishop of Rome, not the Patriarch of the West, that speaks infallibly* ex cathedra, *and it should not be forgotten that at one time the Bishop of Rome spoke in the Greek language.*

In our midst one will find a number of people who desire unity, but they fear Latinization. It is necessary, therefore, to assure them that if the Oriental Church will return to Catholic unity, if she will recognize in the Holy See the power granted and willed to it by our Lord in the person of St. Peter in order that unity, solidarity, and the legitimate progress of Christianity might be safeguarded, she (*the Oriental Church*) *will conserve not only her rite* (*which is understood*), *but also the autonomy of organization and administration as exercised in the East prior to the separation of the Churches.*

To summarize all that was said before, the essential basis for the Reunion of Churches is determined by:

(1) *The distinction between particular opinions of our*

theologians, which can be erroneous, anti-Catholic, and heretical, and the faith of the Oriental Church in its totality, which continues to remain Orthodox and Catholic.

(2) *The distinction between the authority of the Pope as successor to St. Peter the* "Pastor et magister infallibilis Ecclesiae Universalis," *and his administrative powers as Patriarch of the West, a distinction which will guarantee the autonomy of the Eastern Church, without which, humanly speaking, Reunion will be impossible.*

I need not insist upon this point. I have unlimited confidence in the traditional (and divinely assisted) wisdom of the Roman Church and in the superior intelligence and in the particular virtues of the present great Pontiff. It is not a question of defending our rights, but rather a question of accepting his paternal love.

To this I can add but one comment—it is indeed regrettable that, despite the fact that Catholics and Orthodox have so much in common, they are so far apart. Yet, we need not despair, for the day will undoubtedly come when the misunderstanding separating these twin sisters will be removed. For this we have the assurance of our Lord: "I have other sheep too, which do not belong to this fold; I must bring them in too; they will listen to my voice; so there will be one fold, and one shepherd" (John 10:16).

X

BYZANTINE-SLAVONIC CATHOLICS IN AMERICA

FAILURE to write of the American Byzantine-Slavonic Catholics, commonly known as Ruthenians, would leave this report incomplete. But, for many reasons, it is not an easy task to compile the history of this group. As yet, no attempt has been made to collect the rich historical material dispersed among the archives of the Holy See, the Apostolic Delegation, and the chancery offices in this country, as well as abroad. Valuable information is contained in the various newspapers, pamphlets, and almanacs published by leading clergymen, laymen, and fraternal organizations since 1886 for the benefit of the people, and without which it would be impossible to understand the turbulent history of these people and their Church in our land. A brief account of this history was made by Andrew Shipman, the first American who took real interest in the fate of the Byzantine-Slavonic Catholics in America, in an excellent article written for the *Catholic Encyclopedia.*

The Byzantine-Slavonic Church in America owes its origin to Ruthenian immigrants, who began to arrive in this country around 1880. These immigrants came from the Catholic metropolitan province of Galicia, formerly a political province of Austria, later of Poland, and now part of the Soviet Republic of the Ukraine. They also came from the northeastern province of Hungary, later made a part of Czechoslovakia, and now also incorporated into the Soviet Republic of the Ukraine.

Politically, these people were divided into three distinct and heartily inimical groups:

(1) The Russophile faction, a group of Galician Ruthenians who professed Russian Pan-Slav ideals and aimed at a cultural or even a political reunion with the Russian Empire. Because of their Russian sympathies they were suspected of schismatic tendencies.

(2) The Ukrainophile faction, a group of Galician Ruthenians who were in sympathy with a political movement aimed at separating Galicia from Austria and creating an independent state of the Ukraine. In order to emphasize their dislike for the Russophiles and to add greater strength to their separatist movement, they adopted the phonetic

method in writing as against the traditional etymological spelling followed by the Russians and Russophiles.

(3) The Uhro-Rusin (Hungarian-Rusin) factions, composed of Ruthenian immigrants who came from the Hungarian provinces, who preferred to consider themselves politically a distinct group from either of the preceding factions. It despised these and derisively referred to them as "Polaks," while these referred to the Uhro-Rusins with equal derisiveness as "Hungarians."

These political differences, which were constantly and vehemently being aired in the Ruthenian press, often along scandalous personal lines, created an atmosphere of tension and confusion that allowed the Russian Dissident propagandists, financed by the inexhaustible imperial coffers of Russia, to deceive many Ruthenian Catholics who disagreed with the Ukrainophiles. Catholicism was identified with Ukrainism, and as a result a fairly large number of anti-Ukrainians lapsed into schism.

Just when the first Ruthenian immigrants arrived in this country is difficult to determine. However, by 1885 their number in the small coal mining town of Shenandoah, Pennsylvania, was large enough to inspire the Ruthenians with the idea of forming a parish of their own. In response to their petition, Archbishop (later Cardinal) Sembratovich of Lwow, Galicia, sent Father Nestor Volanski, who succeeded in organizing the first Ruthenian parish in America. He was soon followed by others.

The lot of these first immigrant priests was not enviable. They came to a land abounding in strange customs; they spoke no English; their religious customs, unknown to the vast majority of the American hierarchy, clergy, and faithful, caused the Catholics of this country to look upon their Catholicity with suspicion. What most disconcerted American Catholics was the fact that the immigrant Ruthenian clergy for the most part were married men. Furthermore, if we can trust the statements made by these early missioners in their private correspondence, those who could have given some badly needed information to the American hierarchy, such as the Latin clergy who emigrated from those provinces of Poland and northeastern Hungary where Catholics of the Byzantine Rite abounded, misinformed the American bishops about the religious status of the Ruthenian people.

Had more care been shown in carrying out the ancient rules of ecclesiastical procedure, perhaps many of the hardships and misunderstandings experienced by the first Ruthenian missioners could have been avoided. It is true that, whenever the European bishops gave their blessing to priests emigrating to the United States, they also gave them instructions to report to the local Ordinary of their intended mission in order to obtain necessary jurisdiction and faculties. In most cases these instructions were scrupulously observed by the priests. But the European bishops apparently did not realize the fact that the Byzantine Rite was practically unknown to the American hierarchy, that the name "Greek Catholic," the official name of Catholics of the Byzantine-Slavonic Rite, would mislead the American hierarchy and cause them to suspect the Catholicity of these people. The European bishops did not foresee that the American hierarchy had no way of knowing whether the credentials produced by the bearers, even though written in Latin, were genuine or whether the authorities executing the credentials were truly Catholic.

Hence, when the first missioners reported for duty, except in cases when they chanced upon bishops with some knowledge of Eastern Europe, they were received with suspicion. This might have been avoided if these missioners had been provided with credentials from the Holy See, or if the American hierarchy had been informed in advance of their arrival, and been given some pertinent explanations of the differences in rite and discipline. Unfortunately, this procedure was not always observed, even after it was made mandatory in 1892 by a special decree of the Holy See.

Further complications resulted because the European

bishops granted or were understood to have granted these missioners jurisdiction and faculties over the faithful residing in America. As a consequence, a duality of allegiance was created, and the missioners naturally tended to pay little attention to the ratification of these faculties by the local Ordinaries. The American bishops, who were complete strangers to the people, could not enforce their injunctions against the missioners, because the latter always could produce copies of what seemed to be faculties, signed and executed by bishops of the Old World well known to and respected by the faithful.

Thus, in the absence of authoritative spokesmen who could speak on their behalf and who could present their cause to the American hierarchy, the Ruthenian clergy and faithful were left to their own wits. Whenever a dispute arose between the local Latin bishop and the Ruthenian clergy, the latter generally had to depend on correspondence with the Holy See or with the bishops in the homelands. This, of course, took time, and, while waiting for an answer, the parties in the dispute committed tactical errors which deepened their mutual mistrust.

For example, the faithful would approach a local bishop with a request that they be allowed to organize a parish and that the bishop sponsor their cause. The bishop, who often did not understand the lawfulness of a different rite, would oppose the request. Needless to say, this provided propaganda material for the agents of schism.

One of the main points of misunderstanding centered about the holding of church property. According to the discipline enacted at the Provincial Synod of Baltimore, all church properties of Catholics were to be deeded to the local bishop. In practice this meant that when a priest became recalcitrant the bishop could remove him from the parish and enforce the decree that made him sole owner of the property. The early Ruthenian settlers feared that the bishops would suppress their rites and customs as soon as they gained control of their properties. Hence, in many cases, the Ruthenians refused to abide by the ruling of the Baltimore Synod; they incorporated their properties according to the civil laws of the state, thus introducing the Protestant method of holding church property, despite the fact that this was contrary to the ancient laws of the Byzantine Church. In this manner they unwittingly laid the foundation for lengthy and costly lawsuits that were to mark the history of the Byzantine Church in America.

To what extent the local bishops were responsible for creating this mistrust cannot be determined until all documents available are thoroughly studied. At the present time, however, it can be said on the basis of documentary proof that too independent priests made use of every opportunity to deepen the mistrust to their own advantage, and thus escape ecclesiastical supervision and control. These "hirelings," fortunately few in number, who could not be reached by ecclesiastical punishment earned in Europe, created a condition wherein an "electioneering campaign" proved highly fruitful. The condition was the following.

Wherever the church properties were not deeded to the bishop, but were incorporated according to the Protestant system, the pastor became an elective officer; he was thus exposed to the mercy of the members of the congregation. If he became too insistent upon the observance of Church law, he could be voted out of his holding. On the other hand, if a priest became dissatisfied with his own charge and saw a chance to promote himself to a more prosperous parish, by means of intrigue, he could have his fellow-priest removed and could take his place without fear of ecclesiastical punishment.

There were, of course, tactical errors of another order committed by the local Latin bishops, which were magnified out of all proportion. In a memorandum submitted by the Ruthenian clergy to the Austro-Hungarian Government in 1898, the clergy complained that among other things, whenever they invited the local bishop to dedicate a Ruthenian church or cemetery—a function of great importance to the immigrant Ruthenians—he would delegate a Latin pastor to act in his behalf. As yet it has not been determined whether this was a standard practice among the bishops of those days in respect to all churches, or whether it was part of a deliberate policy to keep the Ruthenians under the salt. The Ruthenian clergy and faithful resented this practice, interpreting it in the second sense. Little wonder, then, that in an atmosphere fraught with mutual mistrust and vexation the agents of schism met with many receptive ears.

The first schismatic movement among the Ruthenians in this country was initiated by Rev. Alexis Toth, a priest from the diocese of Presov in Slovakia. According to the decree of excommunication, Alexis Toth had received permission to come to the United States to better his financial condition. If this be true, he was not a missioner prompted by supernatural motives. On his arrival in Minneapolis, he reported to Archbishop Ireland. Just what occurred at this first meeting perhaps no one will know. According to reports published by Alexis Toth, the Archbishop refused to recognize him as a Catholic priest because he was a married man. Instead of appealing from the decision of the Archbishop to the Apostolic Delegation or to the Holy See, Toth defied the Archbishop and took charge of St. Mary's Church in Minneapolis. A lawsuit was instituted to evict Toth from the parish. In the meantime, Toth had contacted the Russian Orthodox Archbishop of San Francisco, petitioning on his behalf and that of the parish acceptance into the Russian Orthodox Church. The schism was accomplished on March 25, 1891, and thus Alexis Toth gained the distinction of being the first Ruthenian priest in America to lapse into schism. By the end of 1898 three other priests followed him into shism—his brother, Victor Toth, who later repented and died in the Church, Michael Balogh, and Gregory Hruska.

At the suggestion of Archbishop Satolli, then Apostolic Delegate to the United States, the Ruthenian Catholic priests called a meeting at Olyphant, Pennsylvania, and on September 5, 1893, elected Nicephorus Chanat to act as their spokesman and vicar. The number of Ruthenian settlements and, with them, the number of churches never ceased growing. Petition after petition was sent to the Holy See, to the Austro-Hungarian Government and to the bishops in the homeland, requesting that a bishop of the Byzantine-Slavonic Rite be appointed over the Ruthenians in America.

Finally, in 1902, the Holy See appointed the Right Reverend Andrew Hodobay, titular abbot and a canon of the diocese of Presov, Apostolic Visitor of the Ruthenians in the United States and commissioned him to investigate the religious status of these people and to submit a report, with recommendations, to the Holy See. The visit lasted until 1906, when the Right Reverend Visitor returned to Europe, discouraged, and as reliable sources report, the victim of slanderous intrigues. His mission, however, won a measure of success, for on May 12, 1907, the Holy See did appoint a bishop for the Ruthenians—in the person of Stephen Soter Ortynski, a great orator and missionary of the Basilian Order.

The newly appointed bishop arrived in this country on August 27, 1907. Unfortunately for him and for the Byzantine Church in America, Bishop Ortynski for a while became identified with the Ukrainophile faction. He was accused of furthering the Ukrainian cause at the expense of the other two factions, and was consequently bitterly opposed by the Russophiles and the Uhro-Rusinians. In addition to this political difficulty the appointment of Bishop Ortynski carried with it certain limitations; these aroused the Ruthenian clergy and gave the disloyal priests and Dissident agitators material that greatly furthered the interests of schism.

Bishop Ortynski did not have full episcopal jurisdiction, but was to act as a Ruthenian vicar general to each local Latin bishop in whose territory Ruthenian churches were located. Consequently, he could not act without consulting the local Latin bishop. Bishop Ortynski was further ordered to promulgate new regulations that the Holy See had issued in the Pontifical decree, *Ea semper*. Among other things, these required celibacy among the American Ruthenian clergy and forbade the clergy to administer the sacrament of confirmation to infants at the time of baptism, both privileges long cherished by the Ruthenians.

The opposition to Bishop Ortynski was spirited, and relapses into schism occurred at an alarming rate. It was estimated that by 1909 approximately 10,000 faithful left the Catholic Church to affiliate themselves with the richly subsidized Russian Orthodox Church. The Russian Government itself let it be known that the Holy Governing Synod of Russia spent approximately $80,000 per year on the Russian mission in America.

The controversy with Bishop Ortynski blazed not only in clerical circles. Overzealous "defenders of the rite" invited the laity, a great percentage of whom could neither read nor write, to participate. This policy proved to be a boomerang, for it quickly undermined the respect and authority enjoyed by the clergy and gave birth to an abundant crop of self-appointed "experts" and "saviors" of the Byzantine Rite.

Almost overnight the Ruthenian settlements were invaded by phalanxes of "priests"—men whom overzealous Russian Orthodox bishops had promoted to the highly responsible priesthood of Christ from the ranks of kantors (organists), real-estate agents (vendors of religious articles), and persons of similar occupations. According to the admissions of Eudokim, the former Russian Dissident Archbishop of New York, of all Orthodox priests actively engaged in parochial work as of May, 1914, only seven had received some higher ecclesiastical education, thirty-five had completed secondary-school education, and the remainder were self-taught.

On May 28, 1913, the Holy See gave Bishop Ortynski full ordinary powers over all Ruthenians living in the United States. A new decree was issued known as the *Cum Episcopo Graeco,* in which the restriction on the administration of the sacrament of confirmation was tacitly withdrawn. This step, together with a compromise by the bishops on political issues, terminated the harmful controversy, as well as Latin resistance to the new bishop. The work of consolidating the Church in America was resumed but reached a new impasse with the death of Bishop Ortynski on March 24, 1916.

To counteract the effects brought about by Bishop Ortynski's change of status, the Russian Holy Governing Synod appointed Stephen Dzubay, a schismatic, as Bishop of

Pittsburgh, with jurisdiction over schismatic Ruthenians. Father Dzubay was transferred from the diocese of Munkacs and labored among the Ruthenians for many years. During the controversy with Bishop Ortynski he grew embittered, and affiliated himself with the Russian Dissident Church. He was consecrated by Archbishop Eudokim on August 7, 1916, in the Russian Cathedral of St. Nicholas in New York City, but his mission as a Dissident bishop was not successful. Later, he repented, was received back into the Church, and lived almost until his death in seclusion at St. Paul's Friary, Graymoor, New York.

Following the death of Bishop Ortynski, the Holy See appointed two Apostolic Administrators: one for the Ukrainians, in the person of the Very Reverend Peter Poniatyshyn, at the present writing stationed in Pittsburgh; the other for all Ruthenians who came from the territories formerly subject to the Hungarian Crown, in the person of the late Right Reverend Monsignor Gabriel Martyak. By this wise, diplomatic gesture the Holy See removed one of the main sources of controversy and dissension. Together with the fall of Tsarist Russia and the stoppage of rich subsidies, it put an end, at least temporarily, to the schismatic movement among the Ruthenians.

On June 15, 1924, two bishops were consecrated to succeed the Administrators: one, Most Reverend Constantine

Bohachevsky, with jurisdiction over all Ukrainian Catholics; the other, Most Reverend Basil Takach, with jurisdiction over all the other Ruthenians, Hungarians, and Croatians.

The long years of disorder and dissension left their ugly mark on the American Byzantine Church. A firm hand was needed to reawaken respect for the laws of the Church. The task that fell to the two bishops was a difficult and ungrateful one, and it was not carried out without many heartbreaks, financial losses, and the sight of repeated relapses into schism.

Hardly had Bishop Bohachevsky begun to create some semblance of order in his ordinariate than the dissenters and the lawless element among the clergy and laity denounced him as a Polish sympathizer, a capital crime in the eyes of every "good" Ukrainian. New disorders broke out; many of the clergy were suspended; and the issues were presented to the people in a distorted way. Soon, the Dissenters found a leader in Very Reverend Monsignor Joseph Zuch. It seems that Father Zuch had left the Catholic Church and affiliated himself with the Dissident Church. He was consecrated bishop, thus winning the distinction of founding the hierarchy of the Independent Ukrainian Church in America.

At the present time, the Independent Ukrainian Church, subordinated to the Greek (Hellenic) Archbishop of New

York, but not recognized by the Russian Dissident Church, is headed by Bishop Bohdan. In 1941 the Official *Directory* of the Greek Church in America gave the names of some forty priests engaged in pastoral work among the Independent Ukrainians, but since that time a number of them are said to have returned to the Catholic Church.

The storm had just begun to subside among the Ukrainians when dissension broke out among the Ruthenians under the jurisdiction of Bishop Takach. This time the promulgation of a new pontifical decree, *Cum data fuerit,* and particularly the enforcement of celibacy, were the pretexts. Chief among the real reasons were the indignation of some individuals at the bishop's attempts to eradicate the abuse of the so-called "trustee system" of property holding; personal jealousies and intrigues; and an attempt on the part of the fraternal organizations to control the policies of the ordinariate.

This revolt started in 1929, and was ostensibly touched off by the papal decree. Numerous lawsuits were instituted by priests in attempts to gain control over ecclesiastical property, including the bishop's cathedral. Several of these priests were summoned before ecclesiastical courts and—the verdicts of guilty having been upheld by the Holy See—six of them were excommunicated by the Holy Father himself.

This schismatic movement, which raged for ten years and is now markedly on the decline, culminated in the creation of another Independent Church, also subject to the jurisdiction of the Greek (Hellenic) Archbishop of New York, but not recognized by the Russian Dissident Church, officially known as the Carpatho-Russian Greek Catholic Orthodox Diocese of the Eastern Rite Church of North and South America. Its bishop is Orestes P. Chornak, one of the six priests excommunicated by the Holy Father, but said to have been consecrated in Constantinople on September 18, 1938. The official Greek *Directory* of 1941 lists forty-five priests; of these one died in repentance, five were originally priests of the Pittsburgh Ordinariate, two were subjects of the Ukrainian Ordinariate, two were converts from the Dissident Church who relapsed into schism, and six were former students of Catholic seminaries.

At the present time, the Ruthenian Catholics in America are divided into two ordinariates or exarchates. One is the Ordinariate of Philadelphia, with jurisdiction over all Catholics of Ukrainian extraction. They have one bishop and an auxiliary bishop, 113 diocesan priests and fifteen religious priests of the Order of St. Basil the Great. According to the latest statistics, there are 305,726 Ukrainian faithful, grouped around 140 churches or chapels situated in the following states: Connecticut, Delaware, Illinois, Maryland, Massachusetts, Michigan, Minnesota, Missouri, New Hampshire, New Jersey, New York, North Dakota, Ohio, Pennsylvania, Rhode Island, West Virginia, and Wisconsin.

They have a preparatory school at Stamford, Connecticut, for boys intending to study for the priesthood, and a house of study for seminarians attending the Catholic University of America, Washington, D. C. More than 187 Sisters, who belong to the religious communities of the Sisters of St. Basil, Sisters Servants of Mary Immaculate, and the Franciscan Sisters, are in charge of the schools. Besides this the Sisters of St. Basil are in charge of an academy for girls and an orphanage, both in Philadelphia. Recently, the Sisters Servants of Mary Immaculate opened an academy for girls in Sloatsburg, New York.

The Ordinariate of Pittsburgh, with headquarters located at Munhall, Pennsylvania, exercises jurisdiction over the Ruthenians from Czechoslovakia, over the Hungarians of the Byzantine-Slavonic Rite, and over the Croats. The Pittsburgh Ordinariate has one bishop, a coadjutor bishop, 147 secular priests, and nine religious priests in the states of Colorado, Connecticut, Illinois, Indiana, Massachusetts, Michigan, Minnesota, New Jersey, New York, Ohio, Pennsylvania, and West Virginia. There are 187 churches and chapels, whose congregations are conservatively estimated at 278,171.

Students for the priesthood are sent to St. Procopius' Benedictine College and Seminary in Lisle, Illinois. The schools are in charge of ninety-six Sisters of St. Basil the Great, the only religious community for women in the ordinariate. The same Sisters are in charge of an orphanage at Elmhurst, Pennsylvania. The motherhouse of the Sisters of St. Basil, in Uniontown, Pennsylvania, is the site of an annual pilgrimage which, over Labor Day, attracts a crowd estimated at more than 30,000. The faithful participating in the pilgrimage receive a plenary indulgence. The festivities offer one of the most inspiring Catholic religious manifestations in this country.

The Benedictine Abbey of St. Procopius, at Lisle, Illinois, is in the process of forming a monastery exclusively for men of the Byzantine-Slavonic Rite. There are now sixteen men at the Abbey, four of whom are ordained priests. The Franciscans are contemplating the establishment of a Byzantine-Slavonic Province within the the framework of the Pittsburgh Ordinariate. At the present time the five friars working in the Ordinariate are priests of the Latin Rite, enjoying a three-year privilege to celebrate the liturgy in the Byzantine-Slavonic Rite. For the time being they are engaged in pastoral work, but it is expected that they soon will be in the position to devote their entire time to missionary work and to the propagation of Franciscan ideals among the Ruthenians.

The ambitious plans of the Ordinariate are hampered by several factors. Until a decade or so ago there were very few vocations to the priesthood. Because of this the Ordinariate could not expand, nor could it undertake any missionary work among the Dissidents. The limited number of qualified teachers among the Sisters of Saint Basil also makes it impossible for the Ordinariate to satisfy the constantly increasing demands for the establishment of parochial schools. The greatest difficulty, however, arises from the fact that, in the absence of a wealthy class of people, the Ordinariate lacks the funds necessary for urgently needed material expansion.

Since there is no reliable census, it is hard to state whether the Byzantine Church in America is increasing or decreasing. As a result, the number of those who have lapsed into schism cannot be estimated. Many faithful of the Byzantine Rite prefer the Latin Rite to their own, but few take the trouble to change their rite officially in the manner prescribed by the laws of the Church. The old accusation that Catholics of the Byzantine-Slavonic Rite "are compelled to use the Latin liturgy"—a slanderous statement unfortunately repeated in the latest official reports of the United States Census Bureau—is today seldom heard.

It would appear that the future problems of the Byzantine-Slavonic Church will be connected not with questions of discipline and rite, but with neo-paganism, with the growing indifference toward God that is menacing all religion in our generation.

XI

CONCLUSION

THE vision of Catholic unity has been the inspiration of many saints and great Pontiffs, it has been the object of many great missions. Yet this truly Christian ideal has failed to materialize, at least so far as the East is concerned, not because it is impossible, not because it is unable to arouse in us a willingness to sacrifice ourselves, but because we have never gone beyond the realm of wishful thinking. We have not buckled down to studying the problem and going about solving it in a practical way.

I do not wish to be misunderstood to say that this failure to accomplish Christian unity in the Near East is due to any malicious omissions on our part. Certain things were done in the past and certain things are being done at present. What I mean is that, if we failed to achieve lasting results, it is because we approached the problem from a wrong angle; we thought we could solve a complicated

Eastern problem by the mechanical use of a Western formula. It is not surprising that, even though there were men on both sides working for reunion between the Catholic and Dissident churches, ardently imploring God to heal this wound on the Mystical Body of Christ, nothing came of these efforts.

The immediate obstacles to this reunion are several, and rather intermixed. One is the difference in language. But the greatest one—the voluminous polemic literature of the Russians gives ample proof of it—is the suspicion entertained by the Russian and Eastern peoples concerning the intentions of the Holy See. And so deeply rooted is this suspicion that even great scholars find it difficult to free themselves of it. Thus, for instance, Emil Golubinsky, the great historian of the Russian Church, fearlessly defied the strict censorship of the Holy Governing Synod of Russia, and insisted on stating the truth even if he had to trample on some of the most cherished, but historically untrue, legends of Russia and her Church. At the same time, when he discussed the pontifical approval of St. Cyril's translation of the liturgical books into the Slavonic tongue, he did not hesitate to risk his reputation as a great and critical scholar by accusing the Holy See of insincerity, when he claimed that the Holy See approved St. Cyril's work only temporarily, to gain the good will of the Slavs, intending to Latinize them, once they were converted to and confirmed in the faith.

Unfortunately for our cause, this suspicion has apparent support in the history of the Church. It is known that shortly after the death of St. Methodius, the Slavonic liturgy was supplanted by the Latin throughout the missionary field of the brother saints. The fact that this was due principally to unfortunate political circumstances, aided by the activities of an overzealous and misguided clergy, and not to the activities of the Holy See, is not so obvious. One needs a thorough knowledge of history and of the earthly functioning of the Church to place the guilt where it belongs.

The Russian polemist did not fail to realize the emotional force of this historical event and, when all other arguments failed, he used it to the full in accusing the Holy See of intending to abolish all non-Latin rites and to supplant them with her own. And in most cases, the emotional argument is the one that finally sways the hesitant.

Consequently, the success of efforts for reunion depends, aside from prayer, on our ability to prove to the Russian and Eastern peoples that their suspicions are groundless. To do this we must present to them, not cumbersome theological arguments that are difficult to comprehend, but obvious historical arguments that will overcome, or at least neutralize, those advanced by the polemist.

And what better argument can we give than to point to a well-organized flourishing Church in which the wholesome traditions of the East are coupled with the faith of Rome in inseparable unity? It was for this reason that Pope Urban VIII referred to the Catholic Byzantine Church in the ancient dominions of Lithuania and Poland as the "hope of the East." Would that all Catholics understood this statement!

We have said that, aside from divine intervention, only a Catholic Church of a given Eastern rite can hope to bring back to the Church the separated peoples of the Near East. Let us look at the record of the Byzantine-Slavonic Church, the largest separated body in the East.

There can be no doubt that Isidore, the Metropolitan of all Russia, was one of the greatest champions of reunion. It was through his brilliance, his power, his prestige, that the reunion at Florence took place in the year 1439. His journey through Europe to his homeland is described as a triumphant march. Yet, barely two years after he had signed the papers in Florence, we see the powerful Metropolitan of all Russia breaking jail, fleeing from Moscow and seeking safety in Rome, leaving the cause of reunion to die a sudden death. Historians ordinarily blame Isidore, yet he does not seem to have been at fault. This doubt becomes confirmed when we consider the records and events which preceded and followed the reunion of Brest-Litovsk, accomplished in the year 1596, to which we owe the existence of the Catholic Church of the Byzantine-Slavonic Rite today. As a matter of fact, the Fathers at Brest-Litovsk accomplished their work so well that nothing could extinguish the newly kindled flame of Catholic unity. Only after several centuries and by conquering them, outlawing them, decimating them, did Tsarist Russia succeed in eradicating the Byzantine Catholic Church from the Russian Empire.

Looking at these two records one asks: Why did Isidore fail where the less prominent, less powerful Fathers of Brest-Litovsk succeeded? The probable reason is: Isidore had only his eloquence to oppose, among other things, to the undeniable replacement of the Rite in Moravia with the Latin Rite. The Fathers of Brest-Litovsk, on the other hand, could put forth an historical argument that was equally strong—which not only added weight to their eloquence, but also supported their claim that the incident was something purely political, and not to be laid at the door of the Holy See. This argument was the reorganized, flourishing Church that combined the faith of Rome and the traditions of Byzantium, holding both equally sacred and inviolable.

In the presence of this argument, the Dissident polemist was robbed of much of his persuasiveness, for all people could see that the polemist was in error when he accused the Holy See of insincerity, and thus doubt was cast upon the correctness of his other arguments. How well Russia and the other nations with Dissident sympathies understood the force of this living argument can be judged from the fact that, when religious freedom was granted by the legislature, the rulers pointedly outlawed the Catholic Church of the Byzantine Rite. Why this exception in the case of a Church which in those days could boast of no power or prominence? The answer is only too obvious. Were the unfortunate peoples of Russia and other nations allowed to see with their own eyes a Church where their ancient and hallowed traditions were not only tolerated, but were deeply respected and used for the sanctification of souls, could these people, by nature deeply religious and anxious for Christian unity, remain deaf to the loving invitation of the Common Father to return to their home? Could these people continue to look upon the Pope, as they had been taught to, as the Antichrist, bent on destroying their religion, their national traditions and their national allegiance?

Many people make the fatal mistake of approaching the problem of the Near East with principles based on a Western mentality, and thus harm the missionary effort of the Church. We hear them stating that true Catholic unity can only be accomplished through unity in rite; when we point to the millions of separated Easterners they lightly brush this argument aside, dismissing the Easterners as ultraconservative ritualists who should be educated into accepting the unity of rites. Now, if we think on this matter seriously, we find that this position is unjust, non-Catholic, and tactless.

Unjust, because the various rites we had and still have in the Church are nothing but the natural external expression of internal belief, expressed in a way congenial to the racial and cultural traditions of the various nations. To preach that only one Christian racial and cultural tradition should be allowed expression savors of the anti-Christian doctrine of racial superiority. The proponents of the single rite seem to forget that the Church's rites, including the Latin one, did not originate in the offices of the Roman Congregations but from the Catholic peoples themselves, and that the Roman Congregations were established only to safeguard the genuine Christianity of these rites.

The single rite position is also non-Catholic (i.e., non-universal) because it hits at the Church's unique and God-given universal character. The Church contains a variety of rites in the unity of faith; to demand that she limit herself to one would be an attempt to condemn her to the status and fate of the Jewish Synagogue, which was established for one race of one particular time.

This position is also tactless, and as such will continue to feed the fires of dissension. For a number of reasons the vast majority of the separated Easterners were very poorly educated in matters of faith. They lived on what was handed down to them by tradition, and as a result were not in a position to distinguish between faith and rite. To them whatever pertains to religion or religious worship is of divine origin and, consequently, unchangeable. Any change in the rite is looked upon as a change in faith; it is looked upon as a heresy which every Christian should abhor. Now, when the Dissident polemist states that through reunion on the terms of Rome the Pope wishes to Latinize the Byzantine Church, one of a Western mentality will interpret this to mean that the Holy See proposes to introduce the Latin ceremonial in place of the Byzantine ceremonial. But a Dissident Easterner will interpret this to mean that the Holy See desires to change his faith—to make him a heretic.

This is no exaggeration. Nikon, the Patriarch of Moscow in the eighteenth century, attempted to revitalize the Russian Church by introducing some needed reforms and by correcting liturgical abuses. In reaction to this reformatory attempt, many of the patriarchal priests and millions of his faithful rebelled against him, denouncing him as a heretic.

They looked on his disciplinary and ritualistic reforms, not for what they were, but for attempts to tamper with the faith of Jesus Christ. In the light of Western culture we might say that these people were ultraconservative ritualists, but in reality their conservatism was a sign of their laudable desire to adhere to Christ and His doctrine.

But, even should a Dissident understand Latinization to mean a purely ritualistic change, in his mind, particularly if he is a Russian, this is tantamount to denationalization, to rejection of his religion. When the Dissidents branded the so-called "Uniates" as traitors and heretics, they were using no empty phrase. To the Russian, rite is the reflection of his traditions, his ideals, his dreams; it is the picture of his soul. To ask that he give up his rite means to him that he must give up his own self.

Unfortunately, history bears him out on this score, too. The Dissident polemist will remind him that in those days when the nobility and upperclassmen of his race, living in the ancient dominions of Lithuania, Poland, Hungary, and elsewhere, embraced the Latin Rite, they also embraced the political ideals of their masters. He will remind him that even today those who abandoned their native rite for the Latin Rite in many cases have become bitter critics of their native rite and of their conationals.

Is it any wonder, then, that we have accomplished so little in this vast, ripe field? Given the circumstances, how can we expect these separated peoples to have confidence in the Holy See, when their polemists can point to clerics and laymen of the Catholic Church who publicly proclaim that true Catholic unity consists in unity of rite as well as unity of faith?

The more the Catholic Church of the Byzantine Rite will flourish, the sooner will the reunion of these separated peoples be effected. Conversely, any injury inflicted on that Church will indefinitely postpone reunion. Would that all Catholics, of all rites, understood.

We cannot penetrate the designs of Divine Providence, but we do know that the Holy See considers the Byzantine Church the hope for the conversion of the East. Looking at the valiant struggle that the Church put up during the past centuries, at that Church's survival despite tremendous obstacles, we find a new and encouraging meaning in the words of Gamaliel: "I say to you, refrain from these men, and let them alone; for if this council or this work be of men, it will come to naught; but if it be of God, you cannot overthrow it, lest perhaps you be found even to fight against God" (Acts 6:38-39).

Some twenty-odd years ago, Bieliaiev, a prominent Russian theologian, undertook to answer some of the arguments advanced by Cardinal Marini proving the truth of Catholic doctrine. His statement can be summed up in these words: Give us an unmistakable sign and we shall believe. Bieliaiev did not deny that one could find saints and great people in the Catholic Church; he did not deny that the Catholic teaching of certain disputed theological questions can be supported, at least to a certain extent, with quotations from the Sacred Scripture and tradition. But he wanted a sign, he wanted assurances that by adhering to the Catholic doctrine he could attain salvation. Is this not an echo of that ancient suspicion?

Read the volumes that deal with the relations between Moscow and Rome and you will read the perpetually-repeated accusation that through reunion Rome is inviting the Eastern Dissidents to commit heresy and to give up their own nation with its tradition, its sorrows, and its glories.

Our Lord did not refuse to give His enemies a sign whereby all could recognize Him as the Savior of mankind; our Lord did not fail to refute the false and blasphemous charges made against Him. And to do so He made use, not of complicated theological reasonings, but of deeds. In like manner, as faithful stewards of the Lord, we, too, must give our opponents an unmistakable sign: we must give them deeds. If we desire to see the day when all Christendom will be one, we must combine ardent prayers with ceaseless and unselfish labor.

And toward what shall we labor and for what shall we pray? Toward removing suspicion and re-establishing mutual trust and love.

BIBLIOGRAPHY

GENERAL

*Attwater, Donald, *The Catholic Eastern Churches,* Milwaukee, Bruce Publishing Co., 1935.

———, *The Dissident Eastern Churches,* Milwaukee, Bruce Publishing Co., 1937.

———, *The Eastern Church,* London, Catholic Truth Society, n.d.

———, *The Mass: Its Various Forms,* London, Catholic Truth Society, n.d.

*Batiffol, Pierre, *Catholicism and Papacy; Some Anglican and Russian Difficulties,* trans. by O. R. Vassal-Philips, London, Sands & Co., 1926.

*Baynes, Norman H., *The Byzantine Empire,* London, Williams & Norgate, Ltd., 1925.

*Bourgeois, Charles, S.J., *Reunion with the East,* London, Catholic Truth Society, 1931.

BYRON, ROBERT, *The Byzantine Achievement, an Historical Perspective, A.D. 330-1453,* London, G. Routledge & Sons, Ltd., 1929.

BYRON, ROBERT, *The Byzantine Achievement, an Histori-troduction to the History of European Unity,* London, Sheed & Ward, 1932; New York, Sheed & Ward, 1945.

*DUCHESNE, LOUIS, *The Early History of the Christian Church,* 2 vols., London, Longmans, Green & Co., 1931 (Especially Vol. II).

*DVORNIK, FRANCIS, "East and West; The Photian Schism: A Restatement of Facts," *The Month,* 179 (1943), 257-70.

———, "Rome and Constantinople in the Ninth Century," *ECQ,* 3 (1939), 409-15.

*FORTESCUE, ADRIAN, *The Greek Fathers,* London, B. Herder & Co., 1908.

———, *The Orthodox Eastern Church,* London, Catholic Truth Society, 1929.

———, *The Uniate Eastern Churches;* London, Burns, Oates and Washbourne, Ltd., 1923.

*HERBIGNY, MICHEL D', S.J., *East and West in the Unity of Christ,* trans. from the French by Mrs. Reginald Balfour, London, Catholic Truth Society, 1928.

Liturgies Eastern and Western: Texts Original or Translated of the Principal Liturgies of the Church, Vol. I, edited with Introduction and Appendices by F. E. Brightman, on the basis of work by C. E. Hammond, London, Clarendon Press, 1896.

MANN, HORACE K., *The Early Russian Church and the Papacy,* London, Catholic Truth Society, 1928.

**St. Bonaventure's Seminary Year Book, 1936* [Twenty-three articles on various phases of the Eastern Church contributed by the students of the Seminary], St. Bonaventure, New York, Duns Scotus Theological Society, 1936.

SCOTT, WILIAM LEWIS, *Eastern Catholics, with Special Reference to the Ruthenians in Canada,* Ottawa, Catholic Truth Society, 1923.

THOMPSON, ALEXANDER H., *The Division Between East and West,* London, SPCK, 1936; New York, Milwaukee, Morehouse Publishing Co., 1936. See review by Dom Bede Winslow, *ECQ,* 2 (1937), 104-5.

TOUMANOFF, CYRIL, "Caesaropapism in Byzantium and Russia," *Theological Studies,* 7 (1946), 213-43.

TOZER, HENRY F., *The Church and the Eastern Empire,* New York, Longmans, Green & Co., 1900.

VASILIEV, ALEXANDER A., *History of the Byzantine Empire,* trans. from the Russian by Mrs. S. Ragozin, University of Wisconsin Studies in the Social Sciences and History, Nos. 13-14, Madison, University of Wisconsin, 1928-29.

WARREN, FREDERICK E., *The Liturgy and Ritual of the Ante-Nicene Church,* 2nd ed., New York, E. S. Gorham, 1912.

WOODWARD, ERNEST L., *Christianity and Nationalism in the Later Roman Empire,* New York, Longmans, Green & Co., 1916.

Periodicals

The Christian East (a quarterly published by the SPCK), London, 1920-38.

The Eastern Churches Quarterly, London, 1936——

The Homiletic and Pastoral Review, New York, 1900——

The Review of Politics, Notre Dame, Ind., 1939——

The Russian Orthodox Journal, Grand Rapids, Mich., 1927——

Sobornost (a quarterly published by the Fellowship of St. Alban and St. Sergius), London, 1935——

CHAPTER I

*Bennigsen, George, "Two Russian Icons," *ECQ,* 1 (1936), 148.

*Dalton, Ormonde M., *Byzantine Art and Archaeology,* Oxford, Clarendon Press, 1911.

———, *East Christian Art, A Survey of the Monuments,* Oxford, Clarendon Press, 1925.

———, *Guide to the Early Christian and Byzantine Antiquities in the British Museum,* 2nd ed., London, Printed by Order of the Trustees of the British Museum, 1921.

*Dirks, Dom Ildefonse, O.S.B., "The Liturgical and Aesthetic Value of Icons," *Liturgical Arts,* 4 (1935), 236-42.

*Fry, E.J.B., "Medieval Wall Paintings in Serbia," *ECQ,* 5 (1944), 249-56.

Hamilton, John Arnott, *Byzantine Architecture and Art,* New York, Charles Scribner's Sons, 1931.

Kondakov, Nikodim P., *The Russian Icon,* trans. by Ellis H. Minns, Oxford, Clarendon Press, 1927.

P., G., "The Hodegetria Eikon," *ECQ,* 5 (1944), 277-84.

Peirce, Harford, and Royall Tyler, *Byzantine Art,* New York, Frederick A. Stokes Co., 1926.

Rice, David T., *Byzantine Art,* Oxford, Clarendon Press, 1935.

St. George, C.F.L., "The Russian Church Art and Architecture," *ECQ,* 1 (1936), 80.

CHAPTER II

*Beauduin, Lambert, O.S.B., *Liturgy and the Life of the Church,* trans. by Virgil Michel, 2nd ed., Collegeville, Minn., Liturgical Press, 1929.

*Bishop, Edmund, *Liturgica Historica: Papers on the Liturgy and Religious Life of the Western Church,* Oxford, Clarendon Press, 1918.

*Dix, Dom Gregory, *The Shape of the Liturgy,* London, Dacre Press (1945). See review, *Theological Studies,* 6 (1945), 554-60.

*Dvornik, Francis, "National Churches and the Church Universal," *ECQ,* 5 (1943), 172-220; reprinted, London, Dacre Press, 1944.

*The Eastern Branches of the Catholic Church: Six Studies on the Oriental Rites, ed. by Donald Attwater, New York, Longmans, Green & Co., 1938.

*The Eastern Churches, New York, St. Michael's Guild, 1939.

FRERE, WALTER H., C.R., *The Anaphora; or, Great Eucharistic Prayer: an Eirenical Study in Liturgical History,* New York, The Macmillan Co., 1938. See review by Dom Romanus Rios, *ECQ,* 3 (1938), 271-3.

*HOFFMANN, ALEXIUS, *Liturgical Dictionary,* Collegeville, Minn., The Liturgical Press, 1928.

*MCGARRIGLE, FRANCIS J., S.J., "The Eastern Branches of the Tree of Life," *Liturgical Arts,* 4 (1935), 181-202.

CHAPTERS III-IV

BURKITT, FRANCIS C., *Early Eastern Christianity* (St. Margaret's Lectures on the Syriac-speaking Church), London, J. Murray, 1904.

*JANIN, RAYMOND, O.S.A.A., *The Separated Eastern Churches,* trans. from the French by Canon Boylan, St. Louis, B. Herder & Co., 1934.

KING, ARCHDALE A., *Notes on the Catholic Liturgies,* London, Longmans, Green & Co., 1930 [Has important bibliography].

*KOROLEVSKIJ, CYRIL, "Liturgical Publications of the Congregation for the Eastern Church," *ECQ,* 6 (1945), 87-96; 7 (1946), 388-99.

*LAFARGE, JOHN, S.J., "Liturgy and Asceticism in the Eastern Church," *Liturgical Arts,* 4 (1935), 218-35.

*MEESTER, DOM PLACID DE, O.S.B., "The Byzantine Liturgy," *ECQ*, 3 (1938), 19-25, 63-71, 131-37, 189-92.

*POTOCEK, CYRIL J., *Cyril and Methodius: Apostles of the Slavs,* New York, P. J. Kenedy & Sons, 1941.

*SALAVILLE SÉVÉRIEN, A.A., *An Introduction to the Story of Eastern Liturgies,* adapted from the French with a preface and some additional notes by John M. T. Barton, London, Sands & Co., Ltd., 1938.

SRAWLEY, JAMES H., *The Early History of the Liturgy,* New York, The Macmillan Co., 1913.

CHAPTER V

BAERLEIN, HENRY, *Over the Hills of Ruthenia,* New York, Boni & Liveright, 1925.

CHAMBERLIN, WILLIAM H., *The Ukraine, A Submerged Nation,* New York, The Macmillan Co., 1924. See review by W. Gurian, *RP,* 7 (1945), 530-31.

CZUBATYI, NICHOLAS, "The Modern Ukrainian Nationalist Movement," *Journal of Central European Affairs,* 4 (1944), 281-304.

———, "The Ukraine, Between Poland and Russia," *RP,* 8 (1946), 331-53.

FRENCH, REGINALD M., *Serbian Church Life,* London, SPCK, 1942; New York, The Macmillan Co., 1942.

GASELEE, STEPHEN, *The Roman Catholic Communion-Uniate,* London, SPCK, 1937. See review by Dom Bede Winslow, *ECQ,* 2 (1937), 105-6.

*GULOVICH, STEPHEN C., "The Ruthenian Tragedy," *The Homiletic and Pastoral Review,* 46 (1946), 574-84.

*HALECKI, OSCAR, "Polish-Russian Relations, Past and Present," *RP,* 5 (1943), 322-38.

MARTIN, DAVID, *Ally Betrayed; The Uncensored Story of Tito and Mihailovich,* with Foreword by Rebecca West, New York, Prentice-Hall, Inc., 1946.

The Orthodox Church in Poland, London, The Polish Research Centre, 1944. See review by Donald Attwater, *ECQ,* 5 (1944), 369.

SETON-WATSON, HUGH, *Eastern Europe Between the Wars, 1918-1941,* New York, The Macmillan Co., 1945. See corrective review by W. Gurian, *RP,* 7 (1945), 531-33.

TESTIS, "Metropolitan Andrew Sheptitsky," *ECQ,* 5, (1944), 343-49.

*TREAMER, AUSTIN, A.A., "A Tour in the Balkans," *ECQ,* 2 (1937), 93-99.

WILSON, H. R., *An Anglican in Estonia,* London, SPCK, 1939.

*WINSLOW, DOM BEDE, O.S.B., "The Catholics of the Byzantine Rite," *ECQ,* 5 (1944), 319-24.

CHAPTER VI

Anderson, Paul B., *People, State and Church in Modern Russia,* London, S.C.M. Press, 1943; New York, The Macmillan Co., 1944. See review by Dom Bede Winslow, *ECQ,* 5 (1944), 367-69.

Arseniev, Nikolai, *Holy Moscow; Chapters in the Religious and Spiritual Life of Russia in the Nineteenth Century,* London, SPCK, 1944; New York, The Macmillan Co., 1944.

Berdyaev, Nicholas, *The Origins of Russian Communism,* New York, Charles Scribner's Sons, 1937.

———, *The Russian Revolution, Two Essays on Its Implications in Religion and Psychology,* London, Sheed & Ward, 1931.

BOLSHAKOFF, SERGE, *The Christian Church and the Soviet State,* London, SPCK, 1942; New York, The Macmillan Co., 1942. See review, *ECQ,* 5 (1944), 93-94.

———, *The Foreign Missions of the Russian Church,* London, SPCK, 1943.

BULLITT, WILLIAM C., *The Great Globe Itself, A Preface to World Affairs,* New York, Charles Scribner's Sons, 1946.

CHAMBERLIN, WILLIAM H., *The Russian Enigma,* New York, Charles Scribner's Sons, 1943. See review by W. Gurian, *RP,* 6 (1944), 247.

EVANS, STANLEY G., *The Churches in the U.S.S.R.,* London, Corbett Publishing Co., 1943. See corrective review, *ECQ,* 5 (1944), 430.

FEDOTOV, G., "Russia and Freedom," *RP,* 8 (1946), 12-36.

*GURIAN, WALDEMAR, "The Foreign Policy of Soviet Russia," *RP,* 5 (1943), 177-93.

———, "Russia and the Peace," *RP,* 7 (1945), 156-69.

KARPOVICH, MICHAEL, "A Forerunner of Lenin: P. N. Tkachev," *RP,* 6 (1944), 336-50.

LOKOMSKI, GEORGE, *The Face of Russia,* London, Hutchinson & Co., Ltd., 1944. See review in *ECQ,* 5 (1944), 431.

*MCCULLAGH, FRANCIS, *The Bolshevik Persecution of Christianity,* New York, E. P. Dutton & Co., 1924.

SOUVARINE, BORIS, *Stalin, a Critical Survey of Bolshevism,* New York, Alliance Book Corporation, Longmans, Green & Co., 1939.

SPINKA, MATTHEW, *The Church and the Russian Revolution,* New York, The Macmillan Co., 1927.

SUMNER, BENEDICT H., *A Short Story of Russia,* New York, Reynal & Hitchcock, 1943. See review by W. Gurian, *RP,* 6 (1944), 249-50.

TIMASHEFF, N. S., *The Great Retreat,* New York, E. P. Dutton & Co., 1946. See review, *RP,* 8 (1946), 409-13.

———, "On the Russian Revolution; Was Stagnation Its Cause?" *RP,* 4 (1942), 287-302.

———, "Religion in Russia," *Christianity and Crisis,* 3 (1943), 2-5.

———, *Religion in Soviet Russia, 1917-1942,* New York, Sheed & Ward, 1942.

———, "The Russian Revolution; Twenty-five Years After," *RP*, 5 (1943), 415-40.

TREVIRANUS, GOTTFRIED R., *Revolutions in Russia; Their Lessons for the Western World*, New York, Harper & Bros., 1944.

VERNADSKY, GEORGE V., *The Russian Revolution, 1917-1931*, New York, Henry Holt & Co., 1932. See review by W. Gurian, *RP*, 5 (1943), 539-40.

*WALSH, EDMUND A., S.J., *The Fall of the Russian Empire; The Story of the Last of the Romanovs and the Coming of the Bolsheviki*, Boston, Little, Brown & Co., 1928.

———, *Why Pope Pius XI Asked Prayers for Russia on March 19, 1930*, New York, The Catholic Near East Welfare Association, 1930.

WEBB, SIDNEY AND BEATRICE, *The Truth About Soviet Russia*, London, Longmans, Green & Co., 1942.

ZERNOV, NICHOLAS, *The Church of the Eastern Christians*, London, SPCK, 1943; New York, The Macmillan Co., 1944. See review by Dom Bede Winslow, *ECQ*, 5 (1944), 266-68.

CHAPTER VII

BIGG-WITHER, REGINALD, *A Short History of the Church of Russia,* New York, The Macmillan Co., 1928.

BRIAN-CHANINOV, NICOLAS, *The Russian Church,* London, Burns, Oates & Washbourne, Ltd., 1931.

BULGAKOV, SERGIUS, *The Orthodox Church,* trans. by E. S. Cram, ed. by Donald A. Lowrie, London, The Centenary Press, 1935. See review by Dom Bede Winslow, *ECQ,* 1 (1936), 67.

*CHITTY, D. J. AND W. A. WIGRAM, *The Eastern Communions,* London, SPCK, 1937. See review by Dom Bede Winslow, *ECQ,* 2 (1937), 106.

CONYBEARE, FREDERICK C., *Russian Dissenters,* Cambridge, Harvard University Press, 1921.

*DANZAS, J. N., *The Russian Church,* trans. from the French by Olga Bennigsen, New York, Sheed & Ward, 1946.

*DUCHESNE, LOUIS, *Christian Worship: Its Origin and Evolution. A Study of the Latin Liturgy up to the Time of Charlemagne,* trans. from the French by M. I. McClure, London, SPCK, 1903; New York, E. and J. B. Young & Co., 1903.

———, *The Churches Separated From Rome,* trans. by Arnold H. Mathew, London, K. Paul, Trench, Trübner & Co., 1907.

FRENCH, REGINALD, *The Slav Orthodox Churches,* London, SPCK, 1923.

HUSSEY, JOAN M., *The Church and Learning in the Byzantine Empire, 867-1185,* London, Oxford University, Press, H. Milford, 1937. See review in *ECQ,* 3 (1938), 182-85.

*ISWOLSKY, HELEN, *Light Before Dark; A Russian Catholic in France, 1923-1941,* New York, Longmans, Green & Co., 1942.

———, *The Soul of Russia,* New York, Sheed & Ward, 1943.

*ISWOLSKY, HELEN, "The Twilight of Russian Culture," *RP*,5 (1943), 356-76.

KLUCHEVSKY, VASILII O., *History of Russia*, trans. by C. J. Hogarth, 5 vols., New York, E. P. Dutton & Co., 1911-1931.

MILIUKOV, PAUL, *Outlines of Russian Culture*, ed. by Michael Karpovich; trans. by Valentine Ughet and Eleanor Davis, Philadelphia, University of Pennsylvania Press, 1942. See review by John Hartog, *ECQ*, 5 (1943), 139-43, and by W. Gurian, *RP*, 5 (1943), 538.

MOORE, BARRINGTON, JR., "The Present Purge in the USSR," *RP*, 9 (1947), 65-76.

*NERSOYAN, TIRAN, *A Christian Approach to Communism*, London, Frederick Muller, Ltd., 1943. See review, *ECQ*, 5 (1943), 228-29.

PARES, BERNARD, *The Fall of the Russian Monarchy*, London, Jonathan Cape, Ltd., 1939.

———, *A History of Russia*, New York, A. A. Knopf, Inc., 1926.

———, *Russia*, New York, A. Lane, Penguin Books, 1941.

———, *Russia and Reform,* London, A. Constable & Co., Ltd., 1907.

———, *Russia and the Peace,* New York, The Macmillan Co., 1945.

PARKER, THOMAS M., *Post-Reformation Developments,* London, SPCK, 1936; New York, Morehouse Publishing Co., 1936. See review by Dom Bede Winslow, *ECQ,* 2 (1937), 105.

ROSTOVTSEV, MIKHAIL I., *Iranians and Greeks in South Russia,* Oxford, Clarendon Press, 1922.

SHULJIN, BASIL, "Kiev, Mother of Russian Towns," *The Slavonic and Eastern Review,* 19 (1939-40), 62-82.

VASILIEV, ALEXANER, "Was Old Russia a Vassal State of Byzantium?" *Speculum,* 7 (1932), 350-60.

VERNADSKY, GEORGE V., *Ancient Russia,* New Haven, Yale University Press, 1944.

ZERNOV, NICHOLAS, *Moscow, The Third Rome,* New York, The Macmillan Co., 1937. See review by Dom Bede Winslow, *ECQ,* 2 (1937), 171-72.

CHAPTER VIII

GORODETZKY, NADEJDA, "A Herald of Slavonic and Catholic Reunion," *ECQ,* 4 (1941), 305-14.

KONCEVICIUS, JOSEPH B., *Russia's Attitude Towards Union With Rome (9th-16th Centuries),* Washington, D. C., The Catholic University of America Press, 1927.

VERNADSKY, GEORGE V., "Reforms Under Czar Alexander I: French and American Influences," *RP,* 9 (1947), 47-64.

*WINSLOW, DOM BEDE, O.S.B., "The Eastern Orthodox and the Anglican Churches," *ECQ,* 5 (1942), 66-72.

———, "The Orthodox and Anglican Orders," *ECQ,* 2 (1937), 1-9; 53-65.

———, "The Orthodox and Edinburgh, 1937," *ECQ,* 3 (1938), 1-14.

CHAPTER IX

BOLSHAKOFF, SERGE, "Russian Religious Thought," *Catholic Mind,* 41 (1943), 40-50.

*HAUSHERR, I., S.J., "The Great Currents of Eastern Spirituality," *ECQ,* 2 (1937), 111-121; 175-85.

*HERBIGNY, MICHEL D', *Vladimir Soloviev, A Russian Newman (1853-1900),* trans. by A. M. Buchanan, London, R. & T. Washbourne, Ltd., 1918.

KARPOVICH, MICHAEL, "Vladimir Soloviev on Nationalism," *RP,* 8 (1946), 183-91.

Orthodox Spirituality, An Outline of the Orthodox Ascetical and Mystical Tradition, by a Monk of the Eastern Church, London, SPCK, 1945. See review by Dom Bede Winslow, *ECQ,* 6 (1945), 127-31.

*PFLEGER, CARL, *Wrestlers With Christ,* trans. by E. I. Watkin, New York, Sheed & Ward, 1936 [Particularly the chapters on Dostoyevski, Soloviev, and Berdyaev].

Second Survey on the Affairs of the Orthodox Church, London, Issued for the Church of England Council on Foreign Relations, by the Press and Publications Board of the Church Assembly, 1937. See review by Dom Bede Winslow, *ECQ,* 2 (1937), 242-43.

*SOLOVIEV, VLADIMIR, *Lectures on Godmanhood,* with an Introduction by Peter P. Zouboff, New York, International Union Press, 1944. See important review by Joseph Ledit, S.J., *Theological Studies,* 6 (1945), 428-35.

*WESSELING, DOM THEODORE, O.S.B., "Vladimir Soloviev," *ECQ,* 2 (1937), 12-26, 65-78, 121-137, 185-202.

ZERNOV, NICHOLAS, *Three Russian Prophets; Khomyakov, Dostoievsky, and Soloviev,* London, S.C.M. Press, Ltd., 1944. See review by Dom Bede Winslow, *ECQ,* 5 (1944), 365-70.

CHAPTER X

DAVIS, JEROME D., *Russians and Ruthenians in America: Bolsheviks or Brothers?* with an Introductory by Charles A. Sears, New York, George H. Doran Co., 1922.

*GULOVICH, STEPHEN C., "The Fordham Conferences," *The Homiletic and Pastoral Review,* 47 (1946), 18-28.

———, "The Rusin Exarchate in the United States," *ECQ,* 6 (1946), 459-86.

HARTOG, JOHN, "The Russian Orthodox Church in the United States of America," *ECQ,* 5 (1942), 20-26.

LEDNICKI, WACLAW, "The Russo-Polish Dispute. The Historical, Cultural and Political Background," *RP,* 6 (1944), 151-74.

MAHR, AUGUST C., *The Visit of the "Rurik" to San Francisco in 1816,* Stanford, Stanford University Press, 1932.

REZANOV, NIKOLAI P., *The Rezanov Voyage to Nueva California in 1806,* San Francisco, T. C. Russell, 1926.

TIMASHEFF, N. S., "The Russo-Polish Dispute. A Study in the Theory of Territorial Settlement," *RP,* 6 (1944), 175-92.

YOUNG, CHARLES H., *Ukrainian Canadians, A Study in Assimilation,* ed. by H. R. Y. Reid, Toronto, T. Nelson & Sons, Ltd., 1931.

CHAPTER XI

BOLSHAKOFF, SERGE, *The Doctrine of the Unity of the Church in the Works of Khomyakov and Moehler,* London, SPCK, 1946. See review in *ECQ,* 7 (1946), 424-25.

BORRON, EDWARD, "Whither Orthodoxy" *ECQ,* 3 (1938), 156-62.

*CONGAR, MARIE-JOSEPH, O. P., *Divided Christendom; A Catholic Study of the Problem of Reunion,* London, G. Bles, The Centenary Press, 1939. See review by M. Bevenot, S.J., *ECQ,* 3 (1938), 46-48, and 3 (1939), 435-36.

———, "Meetings Between Catholics and Orthodox: Some Possibilities," *ECQ,* 1 (1936), 131-35.

*DAWSON, CHRISTOPHER, *The Judgment of Nations,* New York, Sheed & Ward, 1942.

*DICKINSON, P., S. J., "Rome Today and Reunion with the East," *ECQ,* 3 (1938) 215-31.

*DVORNIK, FRANCIS, "The Patriarch Photius: Father of Schism or Patron of Reunion?" *Report of the Proceedings at the Unity Octave,* Oxford, 1942, pp. 19-31.

———, "The Study of Church History and Christian Reunion," *ECQ,* 6 (1945), 17-36.

*MCNABB, VINCENT, O.P., *The Church and Reunion; Some Thoughts on Christian Reunion,* London, Burns, Oates & Washbourne, Ltd., 1937.

*MONKS, JAMES L., S.J., "Relations Between Anglicans and Orthodox: Their Theological Development," *Theological Studies,* 7 (1946), 410-52.

REES, HERBERT, *The Catholic Church and Corporate Reunion. A Study of the Relations Between East and West from the Schism of 1054 to the Council of Florence,* London, Dacre Press, 1940. See review by Dom Romanus Rios, *ECQ,* 4 (1941), 279-81.

*RIOS, DOM ROMANUS, O.S.B., "Benedictine Contacts, Ancient and Modern, with the Eastern Churches," *ECQ,* 4 (1941), 244-55.

SCOTT, SIDNEY H., *The Eastern Churches and the Papacy,* London, Sheed & Ward, 1928.

*WINSLOW, DOM BEDE, O.S.B., "The Encyclical of Pope Pius XII, *Orientalis Ecclesiae,*" *ECQ,* 6 (1945), 1-8.

ZANDER, L. A., *The Essence of the Ecumenical Movement,* trans. from the Russian by N. Duddington, Geneva, World's Student Christian Federation, 1937. See review by Dom Bede Winslow, *ECQ,* 2 (1937) 2-43.

The following abbreviations have been used:

ECQ, Eastern Churches Quarterly
RP, Review of Politics
SPCK, Society for Promoting Christian Knowledge
*An asterisk indicates a Catholic author

INDEX